Public Talk Series: 2

Successful Living

Swami Dayananda Saraswati

Arsha Vidya Centre
Research • Publication
Chennai

Published by :
Arsha Vidya Centre
Research • Publication
32 / 4 'Sri Nidhi' Apts III Floor
Sir Desika Road Mylapore
Chennai 600 004 INDIA
Tel : 044 2499 7023
Telefax: 2499 7131
Email : avrandpc@gmail.com

First Edition : June 2006 Copies: 2000 ISBN : 81-903636-2-X

Reprint : July 2008 Copies: 5000 ISBN : 978-81-903636-2-4

Design :
Suchi Ebrahim

Printed by :
Sudarsan Graphics
27, Neelakanta Mehta Street
T. Nagar, Chennai 600 017
Email : info@sudarsan.com

Contents

Preface

I am very happy to see in print the series of talks I gave in Chennai under different titles for meaningful 'Living'. I enjoyed my reading these manuscripts inasmuch as the material therein was an outcome of my open thinking. In fact in some places I was amused as well as surprised. Anyone who reads this book, I am sure, will find it refreshingly useful. I congratulate the dedicated people at the Arsha Vidya Centre, Research and Publication, for this thoughtful publication.

Swami Dayananda Saraswati
Rishikesh
27 May 2006

Key to Transliteration and Pronunciation of Sanskrit Letters

Sanskrit is a highly phonetic language and hence accuracy in articulation of the letters is important. For those unfamiliar with the *Devanāgari* script, the international transliteration is a guide to the proper pronunciation of Sanskrit letters.

अ	*a*	*(but)*	ट	*ṭa*	*(true)**3
आ	*ā*	*(father)*	ठ	*ṭha*	*(anthill)**3
इ	*i*	*(it)*	ड	*ḍa*	*(drum)**3
ई	*ī*	*(beat)*	ढ	*ḍha*	*(godhead)**3
उ	*u*	*(full)*	ण	*ṇa*	*(under)**3
ऊ	*ū*	*(pool)*	त	*ta*	*(path)**4
ऋ	*ṛ*	*(rhythm)*	थ	*tha*	*(thunder)**4
ॠ	*ṝ*	*(marine)*	द	*da*	*(that)**4
लृ	*ḷ*	*(revelry)*	ध	*dha*	*(breathe)**4
ए	*e*	*(play)*	न	*na*	*(nut)**4
ऐ	*ai*	*(aisle)*	प	*pa*	*(put)* 5
ओ	*o*	*(go)*	फ	*pha*	*(loophole)**5
औ	*au*	*(loud)*	ब	*ba*	*(bin)* 5
क	*ka*	*(seek)* 1	भ	*bha*	*(abhor)**5
ख	*kha*	*(blockhead)**1	म	*ma*	*(much)* 5
ग	*ga*	*(get)* 1	य	*ya*	*(loyal)*
घ	*gha*	*(log hut)**1	र	*ra*	*(red)*
ङ	*ṅa*	*(sing)* 1	ल	*la*	*(luck)*
च	*ca*	*(chunk)* 2	व	*va*	*(vase)*
छ	*cha*	*(catch him)**2	श	*śa*	*(sure)*
ज	*ja*	*(jump)* 2	ष	*ṣa*	*(shun)*
झ	*jha*	*(hedgehog)**2	स	*sa*	*(so)*
ञ	*ña*	*(bunch)* 2	ह	*ha*	*(hum)*

ं	ṁ	*anusvāra*	(nasalisation of preceding vowel)
:	ḥ	*visarga*	(aspiration of preceding vowel)
*			No exact English equivalents for these letters

1.	Guttural	–	Pronounced from throat
2.	Palatal	–	Pronounced from palate
3.	Lingual	–	Pronounced from cerebrum
4.	Dental	–	Pronounced from teeth
5.	Labial	–	Pronounced from lips

The 5th letter of each of the above class -- called nasals – are also pronounced nasally.

TALK 1

Introduction

Any person can say, "I am a failure." However, I have arguments to prove that he or she is also successful. When someone returns home in one piece, he or she is a very successful person. With all the two-wheelers on the road, there is every chance of getting hit. That you come back home intact is in itself a success. When you open your eyes and see, it is a success. A retinal detachment does not take time; it can happen any time. If you look at the emergency ward of a busy hospital, it is always full. Can you ever ask anyone of those patients, "Did you have a prior appointment to come here?" All those people never thought they would end up in the emergency ward. Each one had his or her own plan; one wanted to go home, another wanted to attend a marriage, the third wanted to attend an interview. Varieties of goals were there, but all of them ended up in a place that was neither expected nor desired.

It is a success that we have escaped such a situation all these years. It is a story of success that our eyes still see, our ears still hear, and that the food we eat continues to be digested. We do not know what is in the food that we eat outside, and yet we are able to survive and maintain fairly good health. We have enough reasons to say that we are successful. If you remain married and if your spouse still appreciates the fact that you are his or her partner, which is indeed a great success! If you are employed and your employer thinks that you are an asset, if not an asset, well, not easily dispensed with, that, in itself, is a great success.

Equally, there are enough reasons in everybody's life to drive a person from the society to a life of a *sannyāsin*, renunciate, like me. It is not that people are not *sannyāsins* because there are no reasons for it. Such thoughts do occur because, in our society we have a slot for such a life. An American, seeing my clothes, asked this question,

"What do you do?"

"I do not do anything."

"Do you have a job?"

"No."

"Oh, do you have a bank balance?"

"No."

"Oh, you have a family to support?"

"No."

"You do not have a family?"

"No."

"No job?"

"No."

"No money?"

"No."

"Oh, you are a hobo!"

Hobo is a single word that indicates a person who does not have a job, money or a family. Such a person is a hobo, a vagabond. They cannot place a person like me who does not have a slot in their society.

Suppose an Indian asks me,

"Do you have a job?"

"No."

"Do you have a family?"

"No."

"Do you have any money?"

"No."

"Oh, are you a *sādhu*?"

"Yes."

In our society *sādhus* have a slot, and it is a revered and highly respected slot. Why is there so much respect for this slot? The benefit of doubt is always given to that person. If that person has some difficulties in living a life of *dharma,* then that is his or her problem. From the standpoint of the society, that person who gets into that slot is valued because we consider that he or she represents a pursuit that we all value.

You cannot say that a *sādhu* is a failure nor can you say that he is a successful person. Among *sādhus* we do not know who is a successful person. We do not know whether he is a dropout from society and therefore a *sādhu,* or if he is an adult who has chosen to be a *sādhu,* since both are *sādhus*. A businessman who had lost his business empire, did not have anything left, and who had to repay a lot of loans, said, "I am going to be a *sādhu*." He did become a *sādhu*, and I asked him "What did you renounce?" He said, "All my debts."

Success or failure is a relative term

Just because one is a *sādhu*, I cannot say that he is successful; nor is the person who is busy answering the many phones in his office. Obviously he is doing a lot of work. He answers three phones at the same time. You may think that he is successful and making money. Really speaking, he is answering three creditors who are demanding repayment at the same time. Therefore, we can give enough arguments to prove that everybody is successful and that everybody is a failure. So the word 'successful' is relative. The concept of success itself has to be examined and understood properly.

No one can fulfil one's all desires

Suppose I ask you, "Did you ever have one single day of twelve waking hours totally free from all desires, totally free from the backlog of all your unfulfilled desires?" All of us procrastinate. There is always a backlog, in the office and at home. We have personal letters to write, and we do write every day, but mentally. Then, one day we clear the backlog both at work and at home, and we feel good. Why don't we fulfil all the desires that we have at least for one day? The fact is that nobody can say, "I have fulfilled all my desires today."

As a child you had desires, but not all those desires were fulfilled. Is there a student who does not want to score one hundred percent in every subject? Every student wants to be the best, but settles for something less. Everybody wants to come out with flying colours in every game in which the person participates. Well, you always settle for something less. Anybody who plays cricket or has played cricket fantasizes that he is hitting all six balls in every over for sixes and fours. If you do not hit the ball, you want your man on the other end to hit it. He loses the middle stump. It is always said that Indians do not have the drive to do well. It is not true. When things just do not click, they become hesitant. Therefore, everybody wants to do well. In fact, your desire to do well is so intense that you become nervous.

As a young boy or a girl you had a number of desires that you could not fulfil. You always wanted your father to be a little different, your mother to be a little different. Later, as a young man or as a young woman, well, you had a number of new desires. In fact every young man thinks he has a solution to every problem in the country. His only problem is that nobody consults him. A few more years are necessary for him to become more objective. Once he gets married, then he understands that he cannot fulfil anything; before marriage it was all a fantasy. Everybody has dreams, but then you find that they were not really dreams; they were desires. Later, however, they did prove to be dreams.

At all times there are desires, an innumerable variety of them. You want the people in the society to behave differently, but nothing really changes. I was looking into a particular Tamil newspaper, and I noticed that the page was full of reports of death—somebody died, somebody was killed and somebody committed suicide. The whole page carried only reports of deaths. The second page did not fare better. When I became a *sādhu,* I chose not to read a newspaper for three or four years. Then, one day, I picked up a newspaper. I felt that I had not given up reading one at all; it was just the same old thing. I did not find any improvement or change whatsoever. Even now, the only change I find is this 'dot-com,' every advertisement has one more line now–dot-com; there is no other improvement. Do you know why? Even with the addition of the dot-com industry, you still had desires that people should behave differently, that there should be more order in the traffic, that there should be more *dharma* and so on. People should enjoy whatever they do. There should be dignity of work. You had all these ideals that were never fulfilled. You always wanted the politicians to be a little different. You wanted the world religious leaders to be different, to be more responsible. They should not sow seeds of dissensions, violence by leading people wrongly. So, we find that this problem was there before and continues even now.

Desires are always there at different levels and all of them remain unfulfilled. One way of measuring success is by dividing the desires you had by the desires you fulfilled. The quotient that you arrive at will be negligible. You will see that the desires fulfilled are few and far between, whereas the desires entertained outnumber them. You always have only a fraction of success in fulfilling desires. If that is the concept of success, well, no one is successful.

I am a self-conscious person. Being a self-conscious person I cannot but make a self-judgement and the judgement is that I am wanting. Any which way I look at myself—strength-wise, health-wise, knowledge-wise, memory-wise, morally and emotionally—I am wanting. Money-wise I am always wanting. I cannot command a mind that is somewhat cheerful, if not all the time, at least more often than not. Emotionally, if I am wanting, at least in terms of ethics I would like to be free from conflicts. However, I find that I am wanting, even in these terms.

Therefore, my wanting to be different from what I am is very natural. It is a human urge. Everyone is in the process of becoming. It is obvious that in the different person that you want to become, you want to see a person who is satisfied. Even though you want to change your house, the change is not for the sake of a change or for the sake of the house. It is not that the house wanted itself to be changed. You are uncomfortable in this house and hence want to change the house. So, any change you want to bring about in the society or at home is only for your sake. Therefore, how can one say, 'I am successful' when one is still in the process of becoming?

The wanting you always has so many wants. All of them remain unfulfilled, and some of them cannot be fulfilled at all. Not only do you settle for something less, but your parents also settle for something less.

The parents' desire is that their son should become a scientist or this or that, whereas the child proves to be a Mohammed of Ghazni in the sixth grade! So the parents also have to edit their ambitions with reference to the children. They have to change and reshuffle their ambitions.

At a given time there is a pressure to fulfil a given desire. It becomes very predominant. When you come out of high school your predominant desire is to get admission in a college. College admission is a routine affair in many countries, but in India it is a result of great *tapas,* intense efforts. The most unfortunate thing is that somebody wants to study, but cannot get admission to college without seeking help from politicians.

There is no way you can fulfil all your desires. In this sense everyone is a failure. Each one of us has too many unfulfilled desires. It is very obvious. We want to be successful. We also read books such as 'How to Achieve Success.' Everyone buys that book because everyone wants to be successful. Even the person whom you consider successful is reading the book 'How to Achieve Success.'

It is very clear that as a spouse you are not successful, as a parent you are not successful and as a responsible member of the society you are not successful. In your own self-image, which you can enjoy as a person, you are not successful. There is always a lack in you. So success just cannot be taken for granted.

You always miss what is obvious

Living is successful when you understand what it takes to be a successful person. We always miss the obvious. One unfortunate thing about a human being is that one always misses the obvious. One goes for complicated things. You must have heard about Sherlock Holmes and Watson. Both Holmes and Watson went on a camping trip. It had been a long day and they were tired. They had a good dinner and went to sleep. In the middle of the night, Holmes woke up and called Watson, "Get up."

Watson woke up and asked "Now what?"

Holmes said, "Look up."

Watson looked up. There was a beautiful sky full of stars.

Holmes asked him, "What do you see?"

"Stars and stars."

"What does it convey to you?"

"Every star is a sun and it must have a system of planets. All these stars have planets; millions and billions of planets are there, astronomically speaking. Astrologically speaking, today the moon is in Leo. Horologically speaking the time should be 1.00 a.m. now. Meteorologically speaking, tomorrow will be a sunny day."

Sherlock Holmes listened to all this, paused for a moment, and then said, "Idiot, we have lost our tent, somebody stole our tent!" Like Watson, we miss the obvious.

It is obvious that I continue to be a wanting person. Forty years have passed and nothing has happened. The starting point was 'I am a wanting person.' Forty years later, I continue to be a wanting person. After ninety years, I will still be a wanting person. A ninety-year-old person does not say, "I had a wonderful life, ninety years of a great life." Instead he says, "Swamiji, I am ninety years old. I deserve respect from all my children. Nobody cares for me, nobody writes to me, nobody wants me." Even if his friend wants to talk to him, he cannot, because if the friend just asks him, "How do you do," he starts from his first marriage onwards. In fact the ninety-year-old should be happy that nobody disturbs him and since he cannot go around, he need not knock about. He should enjoy his freedom, for which he should have lived successfully. He misses the obvious.

Here, the obvious is 'I', the first person singular, the individual. I am the obvious. I am the one who is wanting. I should do something about the basic problem of being a wanting person.

To desire is a human privilege

One should know that having a desire is not a problem. Desiring is a privilege. Only a human being can have the power to desire. A cow cannot ask the bullock,

"Honey, shall we eat out today? Let us go to a
restaurant." It does not have that privilege. You
privilege of desiring. Lord Kṛṣṇa, in the *Bhagav*
says,[1] "In the human beings, I am in the form of their desires, unopposed to *dharma*." The capacity to desire is a great privilege really. It remains a privilege only when I am able to look upon it as such. Many of our privileges become sources of problems if we are not on top of them. To live successfully I need to have this understanding, this insight. I need the capacity, in keeping with that understanding, to enjoy the privilege to desire, to act and to accomplish. If I enjoy the privilege of desiring, then I am a successful person.

It is not the fulfilment of all desires that makes me successful, because that is not possible. However, if I begin to enjoy the privilege to desire, to act, in order to fulfil the desires, then I am a successful person. That makes a clean change, a total change, in my attitude towards myself, towards the world, towards varieties of things and even towards the desires themselves.

Desires need not be wants. Desires can be just desires. Not only do you have the privilege to desire, but also to decide. You may fulfil the desire or you may not; you may even just look at it as a fancy and smile away. You need not go after it. Therefore, unless I am able to put the inner house in order, the privileges become tyrants; they become curses. That which ought to make me happy makes me feel I am a failure. Once you know how to put

---

[1] *dharmāviruddho bhuteṣu kāmos'mi bharatarṣabha* (*Bhagavad Gītā* 7.11)

the inner house in order, you can begin to feel that you are successful after all or, that it is possible for you to be successful. We will begin to change.

Talk 2

Discovering Mokṣa As The Prime Value

Lord Kṛṣṇa in the second chapter of the *Bhagavad Gītā* makes a very pertinent statement. He says,[2] 'With reference to the ultimate end in one's life, there is only one well ascertained understanding.' There is only one ultimate end to accomplish if one has really understood, with clarity, what one is after in one's life. I think every human being has to accomplish at least this much. Once we choose an end that is achievable and which cannot be bettered, then the other ends in life will be viewed in their proper perspective, without exaggeration.

Subjective value in money

Everything is useful in the creation. Nothing is absolutely useless. Even a broken timepiece is useful because it shows the correct time twice a day! Everything has its value. Our problem is that we attach more value to an object than its actual worth.

Nobody, including a Swami, can say that money has no value. Money has a value. We respect money. We look upon money as Lakṣmī. We do not separate it from Īśvara. We will discover that there is a reason for it, which is something very beautiful and very significant.

---

[2] *vyavasāyātmikā buddhiḥ ekeha kurunandana* (*Bhagavad Gītā* 2.41).

An average Indian may not know what the *Gītā* is; much less what is said in it, but he or she knows that money should not be desecrated. In our culture, stepping on money is considered an act of desecration. If a person happens to step on it, accidentally, then he or she asks for pardon. Even if you happen to step on an Indian history book that you may not like to read, you will ask for pardon because a book is Sarasvatī, again not separate from Īśvara. This is not taught by anybody. This attitude grows upon one who is brought up in this culture. It is something very significant. It reveals a lot.

Do not take these attitudes for granted. You cannot instil this attitude despite all your media power, all your commercials. It is not easy to build up such an attitude. It is an attitude in our culture, an attitude that has come to be with us because of certain wisdom behind it. Every act, like cleaning the front yard of the house first thing in the morning, drawing *rangoli* is cultural; it is religious and has its basis in our wisdom. Every cultural form in our day-to-day life is connected to wisdom. We may not find this connection between culture, religion and wisdom in other cultures. If there is one such culture, then it is a culture to be preserved.

There are certain facts, certain truths that are not variable. They stand the test of time and can be communicated. If there is a tradition to communicate these truths, and if it is also culturally rich, that tradition is a treasure for humanity.

Thus, money has a value but to add your own value to it is purely, I would say, a projection. In Sanskrit we have a very appropriate word for this psychological projection; we call it *adhyāsa*, seeing something that is not there at all, like seeing a snake instead of the water hose or the rope. On the contrary, knowledge is seeing the object in the given object. There is a flower and you see it as a flower. This is knowledge; it is a perception without error. However, if you see something in an object that is not there, then that is a projection. Psychologically, you project something upon an object and then you deal with the projected object. Here, you have a problem that does not really exist, an illegitimate problem born of your projection.

We can solve an illegitimate problem by realising its illegitimacy. For instance, we can help the person who was afraid of the snake realise the illegitimacy of his or her fear. It takes an extra ounce of care for that person. When you help a person having a real problem, you have not done anything extraordinary. It is a human action. When someone sees a snake where a rope is, and despite telling him or her that there is no problem, he or she is jumping and sweating, then helping such a person does take a little more compassion on your part. Simple human compassion is not enough because you have to solve a problem that does not exist. The only solution is to help the person see that there is no problem.

Every human being is endowed with empathy. Therefore, you always pick up the pain of the other and naturally reach out and help that person. In the process, not only do you get rid of his or her pain, you also get rid of your pain. This is like the psychology of a person given to begging. A begging person who asks, politely, 'Sir, please give me something' will not get anything. He has to persistently plead and pester, in a certain way, 'Sir, sir, sir, sir, sir, please sir, hungry sir, not eaten sir.' It is a time-honoured method meant to disturb you. It makes you feel wretched; you want to get rid of your wretchedness and therefore you give him a coin. The begging person in the street is a psychologist. He knows exactly what he has to do.

One projects due to ignorance. Ignorance is universal. There is ignorance about many things. In fact one is born ignorant— ignorant of oneself and of the world. There is no born-again ignorant; there is only the ignorant who may be born again. We have enough ignorance in spite of our education, our knowledge, and our Internet. In fact the more you know, the more you realise how much you do not know.

The human being is someone who has a capacity, a power not only to know, but also, to project. That you can project is a power and a reality, but then later, you have to deal with that reality, with that mistaken perception. What is worse is the situation where you add a value that, unfortunately, it does not have.

Let us understand more about our projection on money. Money has a value; it has buying power. It is not the paper; the paper is only a promissory note, a bill. However, money does not have the capacity to solve all your problems. Money can buy a book, but definitely it cannot make you read. Suppose the author of a book says, "I will give you this much money to read my book." You will read the book in one day and get that money, but it will not make you understand what is written in that book. Even if there is nothing there to be understood, you should be able to understand that there is nothing there to be understood.

Therefore, you need to look into the value of money. Do not say, "Money has no value." If anybody says so, he has got an eye upon your money. He says, "Money has no value. In earning money there is a problem, in keeping the money there is a problem, and if you lose, it is a problem. There is always a fear, fear of the tax authorities of the State, fear of people who want to rob, fear of inflation. Therefore, give it to me." So money has a value; it is just that it cannot solve all the problems.

Money can provide a very well furnished house, but it cannot make a home. A home is a place where there is communication, honest communication; otherwise it becomes dysfunctional. Without honest communication, everybody walks on eggshells. The father comes home and the people at home become nervous. Each member rushes to his or her room. What a life! Something is drastically wrong in the person's attitude that frightens the children, the spouse. The very arrival of the father is a problem to be dealt with. Therefore, you cannot say you are successful there. You cannot make a home unless you understand what it takes to make a home. It can be a hut, but it can be a warm home. The house can be a palatial building, but it can be absolutely dysfunctional. This is true with reference to everything else that money buys. Everything has a value that is objective as well as subjective.

Subjectivity in relationships

In a relationship, you project all the time. You add a value to the relationship, a value that does not exist; thereby the object of the relationship becomes an object of obsession. Love turns into obsession. Anything you desire becomes a fixation. Mere desires do not remain as desires, as privileges. They become fixations and drive you crazy, causing you to make judgements about yourself and about others also.

We project this subjectivity with reference to people. This is more so in the case of married couples. Let us take a typical Indian marriage. I want you to see this well. You marry a person whom you do not know, although you may have some knowledge of the family. You match the horoscopes because you are entering an important phase of your life. You enter into it with an open mind. Nobody knows how it is going to work. Please tell me now, who or what is it that you trust? Do you trust your parents? Do you trust the other parents? Do you trust the other person? Do you trust your judgement? What do the parents trust?

All of us trust something beyond us, something that is not human. We trust in the goodness of things, in the order of things. This is called trust. It is this trust that is at the heart of an Indian marriage; you have enough space to discover the other person.

You can love anybody in this world. I have seen people who have got rats as pets. You can love a brat also. You can love a cripple. However, when you marry a person in total trust, you discover love which is nothing but understanding. You accept the other person. Therefore, in your trust in the other, you feel secure. Once you feel secure, whatever is in your unconscious will surface and be projected upon the other. The other person cannot understand your behaviour and attitude. This is possible. That is why, after the wedding, for one year it is an emotional roller coaster ride. Of course, you can very well understand that it is not done wilfully by anybody. It is a projection. Many a good relationship is broken because of projection. You see things in the person that are not there; you impute motives to actions and behaviours for which the person is not responsible at all. It is not done consciously, but unconsciously. This is what we call *adhyāsa*.

Therefore, all of us live in a world wherein there is both understanding and projection. You do not see the world as it is available. If you see it, as it is available, you are objective. Only then you can think of any success. Prior to that, there is not even growth.

Reducing subjectivity is successful living

You have to reduce subjectivity. Really speaking, reducing subjective value is successful living.

Subjectivity is fear of sources that do not cause fear, seeing a value in an object that, unfortunately, it does not have. If you are able to reduce this subjectivity, you are a successful person.

If I see the object flower as a flower, like you do and so does everybody else, then this flower is available for public appreciation. However, when you see something, which is not there either in terms of value or in terms of the object itself, well, that is subjective. Therefore, you are in touch with the world only when your subjectivity is not there.

How to reduce subjectivity?

To reduce subjectivity one has to see clearly, first, what is the prime value in life. In our tradition we have the *parama-puruṣārtha,* the ultimate end in human pursuit. *Parama* is the prime, the ultimate, the last value. The last is not in terms of time and order, but in terms of status; it is the cardinal value. What is that value? We say that it is *mokṣa,* freedom. What a word!

All the other religions in the world talk about salvation because they believe that you are already condemned. Therefore, you have to be salvaged; you have to be saved. They talk about saviours. Somebody asked me on the 1st of January, 2000, "Swamiji what is your message for the new millennium?" I said, "I have a prayer: Oh Lord, save us from saviours. In this millennium let humanity discover that they are saved already."

Mokṣa is freedom from what you think you are

We have a value for freedom. The Sanskrit word for freedom is *mokṣa*. It is an amazing word. *Mokṣa* means *bandha-nivṛtti,* removal of bondage. The root meaning is freedom and not salvation. What does the word, 'freedom' mean; freedom from what? You always want freedom from something that you do not like. You may not like certain people and hence you seek freedom from them. That is not the freedom we talk about in *mokṣa.*

Mokṣa is freedom from bondage. The fact that you allow yourself to get frustrated or upset due to someone's behaviour is itself bondage. No one can really bind you emotionally. You give your head, your emotional head, to the other person to allow yourself to get disturbed. Others have capacity to disturb you emotionally only to the extent that you give them the power to disturb you. Physically, anybody can disturb you, but emotionally, nobody has the power to disturb you. You get disturbed to the extent that you give value to the other person's opinion, behaviour, or approval.

Really speaking, *mokṣa* is freedom from being what you think you are. It is not freedom from the world, freedom from people; we do not need it. Freedom is such that you should be free enough to enjoy the world.

Such a person, who enjoys whatever he or she has, is a successful person. He or she has made it. If you have to worry about what you do not have, even if you are a rich person or a highly accomplished person, you will always have a reason to feel wanting. Freedom is enjoying what you are. That is freedom. Freedom is not diversion from oneself.

In today's world, this is the freedom that we seek. We consider the best welfare State as one that is able to provide the most diversions. The more affluent the society is, the more diversions one has in that society. People think that for five days they must work for a weekend holiday. The whole year they work for a long holiday. Their whole life they work for a good retirement. Constantly, they keep looking to the future; they are never in the present moment. Why? It is because they need diversions, diversions not from anyone or anything, but from themselves.

When you telephone somebody and the person is not available, they say 'hold on.' While holding the call, you hear music. Please tell me, why do you have music while holding a call? It is to help you get relief from boredom. Bored with what? You are bored with yourself. Suddenly you are with yourself and you cannot handle this boredom. You cannot stand yourself. There are note pads in the telephone booths that are very revealing. They become thinner and thinner not because you wrote telephone numbers or messages, but because of doodling. Page after page is covered with doodles. Why? You are bored; all the time bored. You are stuck with yourself.

Modern music also reveals how bored we are with ourselves. To enjoy classical music you must have some space inside. Where is that space? Where is that leisure? Where is the understanding? Even to understand, one requires leisure. With modern music you cannot relax; you cannot just sit and listen to music. You have to stand and move about; you 'do' music. You have to divert yourself. Modern poetry is no different. You write a paragraph, type it vertically and call it poetry. Thus, constantly, in various ways, you seek freedom from yourself. Where is the question of success?

You are successful the day you can enjoy yourself as you are. You should be able to enjoy the baldness of your head. You should be able to enjoy your height, your weight, your thinking, and your health or the lack of it. Just enjoy or dispassionately accept the facts as they are. In other words these things do not count at all for your sense of success. You enjoy yourself as a person. I, Swami Dayananda, am not telling this. This is our ancient wisdom, communicable wisdom. Our whole culture, our whole way of life is based upon this wisdom. The unfortunate thing is that we do not know it. If I say that I do not know, it is all right; it is acceptable. However, if I do not want to know, then that is unacceptable. This is the modern method of expression:

"What are you going to do after high school?"

The person shrugs his shoulders and says, "I do not know."

"What about doing medicine?"

"I do not know."

Shrugging the shoulders means, "I do not know," and, "I do not care to know."

A cognitive person is a successful person

To live successfully as a human being you have to know a few things that you cannot afford to be ignorant of. You need a minimum qualification for everything. To be a telephone operator, the minimum requirement is that you should be able to talk and hear. To be a mountaineer, you must have two legs and two hands; that is the minimum. Similarly, to live successfully as a human being you cannot afford to be ignorant of certain facts. You have to know; that is the minimum.

You have to live your life intelligently because basically you are a rational, cognitive and intelligent person. No matter who you are, you have to give respect to that. Nowadays, people seem to have developed an allergy to thinking. They also say, "Swamiji, your talks involve some thinking, at times a lot of thinking." What is wrong with that?

Basically, you are a cognitive person. You have to know a few things that really count in your life. The worst tragedy in life is only one; there is no other tragedy. That the father passed away is a tragedy. The mother passing away is a tragedy. That money is lost is a tragedy. The loss of one's hair is another small tragedy. These are all tragedies, no doubt, but the greatest tragedy is that I cannot think of myself and smile. When I think of myself I pull a long face. I begin to whistle a song. A person is driving a car and gets into a traffic jam. He gets upset and is cursing everybody on the road. Then suddenly he begins to sing. Do you think he sings because he is ecstatic about the traffic jam? No. He begins to think of himself. Some sadness, some inner pain surfaces. He wants to divert himself from himself and the music comes in handy.

Therefore, you cannot just think of yourself and smile, a smile that is an expression of contentment, of satisfaction, of just being what you are. If you can, then you will find that everything else you have is an addition to your success. Any accomplishment becomes an additional luxury.

Our forefathers lived a very simple life, perhaps in huts with a couple of bullocks and buffaloes. This was their life. They did not go to a school or a college. They were not under pressure to score ninety-nine and a half percent to get admission to a college. All these neurotic situations were not there for them. These were our forefathers and that is why we are still sane today.

It looks to me that progress in terms of modern civilization still has a long way to go. Our forefathers were perhaps not civilized, in a certain way. They did not have toothbrushes; instead they may have used twigs. We, on the other hand, are civilized now.

Civilization is converting luxuries into necessities!

What is civilization anyway? Any improved thing that you get is always a luxury in the beginning.

When I was a boy in the village, all of us used to walk barefoot to school. One boy got a pair of shoes and for him it was a luxury. On rainy days, the roads became slushy. Then, this boy would remove the shoes and carry them on his head. The pair of shoes was a luxury for him. Later, when everybody had shoes, it was no longer a luxury. Once you get used to wearing shoes, they become a necessity. The first time that you get a bike, it is a luxury. You take good care of it by wiping and cleaning it. Once you get used to it, then without a bike you have no mobility. You do not even think about the bike, it has become a necessity. Similarly, you buy a car. At first, it is a luxury, but soon becomes a necessity. The air-conditioner, you have, is a luxury at first then it becomes a necessity.

Therefore, civilization is converting luxuries into necessities. The more civilized you are the more luxuries you have converted into necessities. This is an observation of a fact, but it does not mean that I want you to change. Continue to enjoy whatever you have. I am just examining the truth of this civilization. The more luxuries you have, the more freedom you have with reference to them. You can be happy even without these luxuries, but if you cannot, then the luxuries become necessities.

Therefore, we have hundreds of necessities. I would say necessity is like a woman who, at first, is a guest in your house. You can be without her. After some time, she makes herself indispensable. Without her the house cannot run at all. This is what has happened to us, we have more necessities. Outwardly, we are civilized, perhaps, but really speaking, inside, we are strangled completely. Each one is strangled in himself or herself as a person because there is no self-approval.

In self-approval everything becomes a luxury

Suppose, you are able to discover something, so beautiful, so complete and profound about yourself, that it makes you completely acceptable to yourself, then, everything else becomes a luxury. Your mind is a luxury, your body is a luxury, your pursuits are luxuries, your successes, well, all of them are luxuries. Everything else is a plus because you are at home with yourself. If you look at yourself as an unacceptable person, then you have to re-look into yourself.

Positive thinking is not the solution

Positive thinking will not help here, only right thinking will. I always tell this story to prove this point. This person was doing his doctorate, but his thesis was not coming out well. In the meantime he took up a job as a lecturer in the local college. He liked the job, but his Ph.D. was still incomplete. Then, he got married, was happy and well settled in life. Everything was fine, until his friend, who was also doing his Ph.D., was appointed as the Head of his department. All his feelings of 'being happy and well-settled' vanished. He started feeling, 'I am a failure, I should have finished my Ph.D., I did the wrong thing, I ought to have completed it.' He became very depressed and went to a therapist. The therapist, who thought of himself as a very positive person, had one type of therapy, positive thinking therapy. He asked this person,

"How many blind people are there in the world?"

"There are millions."

"Are you a blind?"

"No."

"Should you not be grateful for having good eye-sight since you have 20/20 vision? Is it not wonderful?"

"Maybe, I should be grateful."

"Are you deaf and dumb?"

"Not at all."

"Do you know how many people are deaf and dumb?"

"Yes I know."

" Should you not be grateful?"

"Yes, I should be grateful."

"Are you on a wheel chair?"

"No."

"Should you not be grateful? So many people are on wheel chairs."

"I think so."

"Are you not educated?"

"Yes. I am educated."

"Should you not be grateful? There are millions of people who are not educated, who cannot read, who cannot write. You have a Master's degree, my God! What a qualification you have! Should you not be grateful?"

The person started feeling better. "Yes, yes, I think I should be grateful."

"Are you not married?"

"Yes I am married."

"Should you not be grateful?"

"For what?"

"That she still thinks you are wonderful."

"Ah, I think I should be grateful for that."

"And you have a job, should you not be grateful?"

"Yes, I think I should be grateful to the powers that be. I think I have been thinking wrongly."

"Ah, think positively; you have so much."

The person felt so good, walked out smiling and just then a new Mercedes car stopped in front of him. He saw a man getting down from the car and standing on his legs. He had eyes, did not even wear glasses and was not deaf and dumb, as he was talking to someone. He had everything plus a Mercedes. All the positive thinking vanished. He was depressed again. Do you know why? It is because it is a fact that he does not have a Mercedes.

He has an old dilapidated Ambassador car whose spare parts you can hear. Except for the horn every other part is heard. When he goes to his car and opens the door he needs help to open it. How can he retain his positive thinking when what he does not have is a grinning reality, a teasing reality? It is a reality that makes him feel, 'I have not made it.' All his positive thinking evaporates. Positive thinking may be helpful to face an interview. In life it is not going to help because what you want to have and do not have is a reality. What you have, of course, is a reality.

In fact, the reality is that in spite of what you do not have and what you have, you are someone who is to be reckoned by yourself as a person. It is not positive thinking, but just thinking, objective thinking. It is recognising what is. This is wisdom.

Without this wisdom, we have a lot of projections, not only upon things outside, but also projections within ourselves. Unless the basic projection that is inside is taken care of, we cannot take care of any other projection. We have to look into this very thoroughly.

Talk 3

Happiness Is Centred On The Self

It is very funny to say that you have to free yourself from yourself. We always think that we are tethered by a number of external factors; but basically you loathe yourself. This is a very humbling discovery. You are not able to approve of yourself as you are. The constant attempt, therefore, is to be different from what you are. In the process of this becoming, you create more problems for yourself and naturally for others also.

There is a statement in the Taīttirīya Upaniṣad:[3] "Why did I not do the right thing? Why did I do the wrong thing?" Even if you forget to notice or do not take them seriously, you always have someone around to point out your omissions and commissions. Your own omissions and commissions leave you guilty, while the omissions and commissions of the 'significant others' in your life cause you hurt. 'Why did he or she not do this for me or why did this person do this to me?'

You are the subject and you are also the object. As the subject of action you are guilty and as an object of somebody's action you are hurt. Therefore, for the

---

[3] *kimahaṁ sādhu nākaravam, kimahaṁ pāpam akaravam iti* (*Taīttirīyopaniṣad* 2.9).

self-conscious person the guilt and the hurt are naturally against himself or herself as a person. The *Gītā* says:[4] "One is an enemy to oneself." One becomes an enemy to oneself because one loathes oneself. Positive thinking is not going to help one here.

Everything is a privilege if there is self-acceptance

You have to see yourself as acceptable to yourself. If you do, then you are a free person. Everything becomes a luxury. Your mind is a luxury, because even without thinking you are satisfied with what you are. Thinking becomes a privilege. Without willing you are happy being yourself. Willing becomes a privilege. Without remembering, recollecting, you are happy being yourself. Recollecting, remembering becomes a privilege. Without desiring anything you are happy, desires become privileges; you are free to have a desire or desires. In the very self-awareness, there is a satisfaction.

Your physical body is a privilege. Its limitations do not really count if you are a satisfied person. This is called freedom. One is free enough to have a limited body, a limited mind or a set of senses with their limitations. Everything else that is external is a plus for you. This freedom is not relative. A relative freedom is always variable because you are free only for a moment—when you forget yourself as a person who is not acceptable. Therefore, relative freedom results in only relative happiness.

Happiness is not an object nor an attribute

Happiness cannot be a particular object. If it is, then all of us can keep it with ourselves. Happiness is neither an object nor an attribute to an object. A leaf is an object. When you say, 'green leaf,' green is an attribute to the leaf. Similarly, there is no object called the happy object that has the discernible attribute 'happy,' like the colour green. Happiness is neither an attribute that is visible nor is it a substantive. There is no particular place that can make you happy or unhappy. In fact, any place can make you both unhappy and happy. There is also no particular time you can call as the happy time. You cannot say at 5.00 p.m., every day, you become happy. It means that the rest of the time you are not happy. That is not true.

You cannot call relationships as happiness. Every relationship has its own friction. This is all we have in the world—time, place, objects, attributes and relationships—and none of them can be called happiness.

You need not fulfil a desire to be happy !

In spite of this, occasionally, you find that you are happy. Since occasionally you are happy, you do understand one thing very clearly; that this happiness is not due to something, is not even due to an effort; it is in spite of you. If you become happy in spite of all the unfulfilled desires, should it not enlighten you to the fact that that you need not fulfil desires to be happy? If you have to fulfil every desire to be happy you cannot discover a moment of joy in your life.

The pending desires are too many. Consequently, the ongoing desires also remain unfulfilled. Then, when are you going to be happy? Someone said, "When you fulfil a desire you become happy. In fact, happiness is between the fulfilment of a desire and the rise of another desire." This is not true. There is no guarantee that one will be happy after the fulfilment of a desire. In fact, sometimes one has regrets after fulfilling a desire. Perhaps one wanted a particular job; one joins it only to discover it was the wrong thing to do. Therefore, there is no guarantee that every time you fulfil a desire you become happy. Further, there is no such rule that you can be happy only when you fulfil a desire.

Once, I read a hoarding in Mumbai. It was a hoarding promoting Standard Battery. There was a question, "Why is a mother-in-law like a Standard Battery?" The answer was given below, "Because she goes on and on and on and on...." (laughter). Please tell me, which desire did you fulfil? Did you get your tenant evicted when you wanted the house for yourself? Did you get rid of the squatter on your land? Did you pay all your credit card dues? Did you collect the money that you had lent? Did your finance company give you back your deposits? Did you get all the hair back on your head? Did the politicians undergo a total change? Did the clergies of different religions realise their responsibilities? What desire did you fulfil? None. All the desires are still there. Some of them do not seem as though they can be fulfilled at all. At the same time you are able to discover a moment of joy. This only proves a point. You need not fulfil a desire in order to be happy.

Happiness is centred on yourself

This is not an ordinary fact. You need not change anything. Yet, at the same time you can discover amoment of joy without fulfilling a desire. More often than not, you find that the moments of joy you pick up in your life occur when you do not fulfil any desire. For the time being, your attention is caught by a situation that draws you away from your notions of yourself. The self-loathing attitude towards yourself dissolves for the moment and therefore you are happy.

Happiness rests neither within you nor outside you. The outside world cannot deny you happiness, nor can it create happiness for you. It can only provide situations wherein you can be happy. Much less does your mind create happiness for you; yet, you find yourself happy. When you see a flower, you relate to it as an object and say, 'this is a flower.' And similarly, this is a Swami, this is a chair, this is a tree and so on. However, you cannot point to something and say, 'This is happiness.' You relate to happiness as, 'I am happy,' or 'I am not happy.' That means the fact of your being happy or not happy is centred on yourself. Hence, there is no reason for you to say that you are not successful at all. If you think you are successful only if all your desires are fulfilled then, indeed, you are a failure.

As a teacher, my job is only to bring your attention back to yourself. Without fulfilling any of your desires, if you can be happy, if you are acceptable to yourself, then you are well set. You have a very meaningful journey ahead of you. This is what is meant by the Sanskrit word, '*mokṣa*', freedom; freedom from the notion of what you think you are. Technically, we say it is *saṁsāritva-nivṛtti*, freedom from the mistaken notion about oneself that one is limited and unhappy. This freedom is not merely a hope, but an insight that is more than a hope. Your own experience of happiness gives you an insight about yourself and it is not just a hope anymore.

The notions about oneself are not intrinsic to the self

When you see the sun covered by clouds you do not conclude that there is no sun. The very fact that you see the clouds reveals that there is a sun. The silver lining around the clouds also reveals the existence of the sun. You will see the sun, however cloudy the sky is, for the clouds are not stationary; they keep moving. As one body of clouds moves away and the other body of clouds is yet to close in, you see the sun in between.

Similarly, despite all your tensions, disappointments, sense of failures, and your judgement about yourself that you are no good, you find that you are happy. This is so because all these notions are variable and are not intrinsic to the self. They are only thoughts and cannot stay, since they do not have a foundation, a basis. Being variables, they move away and you recognise yourself as a happy person. A happy person is one who is not afraid of the world and who is free from the notion of insecurity.

Whenever you forget yourself, you are happy. Suppose I ask the question "When do you want to be happy?" You are not going to say, "I want to be happy tomorrow, today I am ready to be unhappy." Perhaps, as a bargain, you may accept, "Swamiji, I am ready to be unhappy today, but make sure that at least I am happy tomorrow." Therefore, where is your heart? Is it in unhappiness? No, your heart is always in happiness. You want to be happy now and forever, in all places and in all situations. If this is so, then you have to assume that this happiness, which you experience at certain moments despite all your desires, must have a certain truth, and that should make the self totally acceptable. Thus, one gains an insight into the problem of insecurity.

Securities do not solve the problem of insecurity. Money, power, influence, name, health, friends, all these create a sense of security. There is nothing wrong in having them. I do not say that you should give up any of them. However, you should know that as long as these are necessary for you to be secure, you are insecure.

Everyone wants to be free from crutches

Nobody holds on to crutches for fun. Suppose someone had a fracture and had to use crutches for three months. Then, one day the person is able to walk on his or her own. The doctor says, "Now you do not need crutches any longer. You can walk on your own."

The person, however, insists, "Doctor, I have been using these crutches for the past three months. I am in love with them. I would like to use them forever." Nobody would like to have crutches. It is human nature to want to be free.

Everybody wants to be on his or her own legs, to be independent. This is what we call 'standing on your own legs.' You learn it even from childhood. At first, a child needs something to hold on to. Later, as it grows, it learns its sense of balance and has the power to stand on its own. It does not need crutches any longer. The love is always for freedom, freedom from crutches. Therefore, if money gives you a sense of security, you accept it, but at the same time, it reveals your basic insecurity.

As a person, you are aware of your deep sense of insecurity, your sense of incompleteness. Therefore, you seek something secure to make you feel complete. You want to be different from what you are; you want to be approved of by others and actively seek everybody's approval. However, the others also seek approval from you. Both are seeking mutual approval and we do grant it sometimes, but conditionally.

My attempt here is to make you see that you seek approval because you do not approve of yourself. That is the reason why, if somebody says that you are wonderful, you always question, "Do you really think that I am wonderful? What makes you say so?" This is because there is self-doubt. You do not totally approve of yourself.

Therefore, let the goal be very clear to you. The self has to be totally acceptable to you. Let the whole humanity say that you are no good; if you see yourself as good, then there is no question of any confusion. If the whole humanity were to tell you that you are not a human being, would you begin to doubt it? Are you going to check if you have a tail? Even if the whole humanity is crazy enough to tell you so, you will only say that humanity has gone crazy. This is knowledge. You are not going to buy others' ideas. What others think will not mean anything to you as long as you think properly about yourself.

The problem is you, the solution is you !

In the vision of our *śāstra* the self is totally acceptable. You sense this whenever you experience a moment of joy. In a moment of joy it is very clear that you are secure, you are happy. The world has not changed. The stars, the sun, the earth, the people, everything is the same. Nothing has changed, and yet, you are able to laugh heartily. The reason is that you see yourself differently when you are happy. In fact, you see yourself as the person you want to be. What you want to be is the person that you already are. That is why, I say, you are the problem and you are the solution.

If this is so, then, this freedom from self-non-acceptance and self-confusion is what is called '*mokṣa*.' It is entirely different from going to *svarga*, heaven. Most religions are promoters of tourism asking you to go to heaven. We look at this heaven purely as a holiday out, a 'get away from it all' vacation. If there is no self-approval then one can remain sad even in heaven. Going to heaven is not *mokṣa*. *Mokṣa* is here and now. Right now, one has to know the truth of what is.

One thing is definite: our problem is not other than ourselves. Therefore, nobody will come to save you. You are the saviour of yourself. In fact, you do not need to be saved. You are already saved, because you cannot be more than what you are.

Modern science has proved the fact that everything is a manifestation. When you look at the sky, you see the stars twinkling at a distance. The light of the stars takes thousands of years to reach the earth. With the Hubble telescope you can even see the star whose light began travelling twelve billion years ago. Yet, there are people who say that the world was created two thousand years ago.

A well-educated Baptist once argued with me in California. This was an interesting episode. His argument was that this world was created three thousand years ago.

I said, "What are you saying? What about all these Dinosaur's skeletons that are millions of years old, whose existence has been proved by carbon testing?"

He said, "We do not accept the carbon test."

"Who are you to accept it or not. The carbon test is a proven test."

Then he asked me a question, "Do you accept that God is almighty?"

I said, "Yes."

Then he said, with that special smile, "If God is almighty, then was it not possible for him to put a few skeletons when he created the world three thousand years ago?"

I asked him, politely, "Sir, how will you have your coffee, with or without milk?" (laughter). I realised that it was useless to talk to him further.

How can one say that the world was created three thousand years ago? I do not know how they continue with this notion against all evidence. If, against all evidence and against all science, somebody were to persist and be committed to a belief system that is blatantly wrong, well, that person's head has to be sympathised. This is a psychological problem. The evidence is so glaring. Science has already proved beyond doubt that the world is not just a creation; it is more a manifestation. All that is here is nothing but quantum objects; it is all particles.

If everything, including an electron, is a quantum object, then, who is the person who is conscious of the electron? That person is being discussed in our *śāstra* as the person who is the content of everything and who is the answer to what we call the human predicament.

The human predicament is due to his being self-conscious. If the self-consciousness were not there, there would be no self-judgement, no complex, no problem of becoming, no problem whatsoever, except the problem of survival as a living organism. There is a self-judgement, however, and in that judgement the self should be approvable, otherwise one is not going to accept or approve of oneself as a person. Such self-approval is experienced by you, but not recognised. The self is approved of when you experience moments of joy, when you are happy with the world, with yourself, with everything. You are the solution; nothing less can you accept. Therefore, *mokṣa* is not a trip. It is freeing yourself from your notions. This is what we call spirituality.

What is a spiritual life ?

A religious life is not a spiritual life, whereas every spiritual person lives a religious life. A spiritual person cannot really become spiritual without being religious. Being religious is not just religiosity. It is to understand Īśvara. You settle accounts with Īśvara; we will soon look into what is Īśvara. People who have a set of beliefs, and who pursue it only to go to heaven, need not undergo any change whatsoever. All they need is to just live with their beliefs and die with them. This is a religious life.

In India, the religious, spiritual, cultural and social aspects of life are all closely connected. The fact is that everything is connected to the spiritual life, but we have to know it. We have forms, but we may not know the content. Spirituality helps us to see the spirit behind those forms. A spiritual life is recognising the fact that you are the solution. You have to know yourself as the truth of everything. If this is the goal, then your life itself becomes spiritual. This is called *vyavasāyātmikā buddhiḥ*, clarity with reference to one's goal, understanding that one seeks nothing else except freedom from insecurity. You are not seeking security, but you are seeking freedom from insecurity. Freedom from insecurity is the security and that is what you are. Our *śāstra* says that there is nothing more secure than yourself. Everything else has its being in you alone. What a vision! You are the most secure. That you have no problem is a challenge for you. You say, "Swamiji, I want to be saved, I want to be saved." But, you are saved already!

Mirabai says in one of her songs: "I went to the *guru*; I saluted and pleaded with him to save me. Do you know what he did? He turned my eyes towards myself. I came to my *guru* to be saved, to cross this ocean of becoming. Lo and Behold! I found that there was no water under my feet." What a wonderful song! We have this vision; it is everywhere. In our songs, in our literature, in all our languages, be it Tamil, Hindi, Telugu, Gujarati, Assamese or any other, the vision is very much there.

You are successful when the end is clear to you

The ultimate end must be very clear to you. Once the end is clear, I tell you, you are already successful. There is no reason for you to conclude that you are not successful because you are the end. It is a question of your owning up; it is a process of learning and gaining clarity of the vision. That insight itself is amazing.

I will give you that insight with an incident. It is a village scene. One Subramaniam, affectionately called

Subbu, inherited a lot of money. He was neither working nor wanted to work. He spent his time idling, constantly chewing a betel-leaf. He lived only to eat. It was just impossible to cook for him. He used to throw tantrums and fling the plates if the salt in the food was slightly more or slightly less for his taste. When one lives to eat, then eating becomes the only committed project. In the morning he would talk about the lunch menu; at lunch he would talk about dinner and at dinner he would decide what he would have for breakfast the next morning. No cook could satisfy him. He was always angry. The lady next door asked me to do something about this. I talked to Subbu and found out that he could sing and had a good voice. I told him, "You have a very good voice. You are gifted."

"Really, really Swamiji?"

"Yes, you have good voice and a talent for music."

"Do you think that I can learn music?"

"You should learn music and there is a musician already nearby."

Subbu started learning classical music and slowly it caught hold of him. Because he loved music, after a few months, he was singing while eating, while walking, even in between, in short, all the time. It was no longer a problem to cook for him. He realised that music is a much more profound and aesthetic pleasure than eating. This is change.

The vision of the śāstra changes one's priorities

This is what we have to undergo, a transformation, a change. The change is not from the role of the officer, the husband, the wife, the father, the mother, the mother-in-law, the daughter-in-law; the change is you, the basic person who is playing all these different roles. When you change your whole attitude towards yourself, you are successful.

This change is like the big signboard in the transit lounge at London Airport. It is very interesting to watch it. On the signboard there are names of different Airlines such as Air India, British Airways, Air Canada, Air France, KLM and so on. At the start, Air India was not there at all. Then Air India appeared at the bottom of the signboard with its scheduled departure time. When the information on the signboard changes, there will be a sound '*gada, gada, gada gada*' to attract your attention. Otherwise one generally sleeps while in transit and misses the flight also. Now, there is the sound '*gada, gada, gada, gada*' and you find Air-India that was at the bottom has gone up by one step because British Airways at the top has taken off. After sometime, again you hear the sound, '*gada, gada, gada, gada.*' Now Air Canada is there on the top. Then you find Air India also climbing up to the top slot and soon, it is ready for boarding. '*Gada, gada, gada, gada,*' and Air India takes off. A similar '*gada, gada, gada, gada*' has to unfold in your mind also. Priorities have to change; a shift takes place for a take off.

You need not change anything. You need not change your job; you need not go to an ashram; you need not go anywhere. You change just being where you are. Priorities change for a take off. This is successful living. Our *śāstra* gives you that vision, gives you the hope. Not only hope, it points out your experience and reveals what it is. What else do you need? You do not need anything else. No assurance is required.

Therefore, once this change takes place in your mind, you prioritise your goal. Then, everything else becomes subservient to this goal. There are no failures. This is wonderful! You can accomplish a number of things in your life. Relatively speaking, you can also accomplish the relative concept of success. Basically, however, you should be able to see that you are the solution.

There is nothing better than the discovery of what I am. Whenever you are happy you are the whole. It is the wholeness that you experience which is called happiness. That wholeness is your nature. You have to know this. That is why, being happy you are at home. You do not complain: "These days I am happy, I do not know why I am happy." It is natural to be that whole person. We will look into this whole person and into the relative concepts of success.

Talk 4

You Are The Whole

We have already seen that there is no possibility of anyone becoming happy if one has to fulfil desires in order to be happy. We also saw that in spite of one's desires, wants and struggles, one does see oneself full and complete in moments of joy. We must see the implications of that moment. We generally gloss over the implications. That is our problem. People say that we learn from experience. I wish we did. We hardly learn. Unless our attention is turned to the implications we will always assume a stance, the stance of a 'ninja.' A 'ninja' is a mythological fighter or perhaps he was a fighter once. He has hundreds of weapons. He has swords, a bunch of *cakra*s, discs, that he knows how to throw and if that is exhausted then he has a bunch of nails that he can use. He has smoke bombs, ropes and so on. He can jump all over. He can even do karate. A ninja fighter is one who does not give up. If you think that he is dead, as you walk away, he gets up. He is a 'never say die' person.

Every human being has this stance against the world. If you know some astrology, then you take a stance against the stars and planets. You think that they all conspire against you. The fear, the sense of being persecuted by every force, every person and every bug makes you assume the stance of a fighter.

A moment of happiness implies 'you are the whole'

The implication of a moment of happiness is this: the very world to which you are alive, that is full of snares and threatening situations, seems to be perfect. The moment you have a complaint against the world, you can no longer be happy. Your happiness is edited and abridged to the extent of the complaint, the severity of the complaint. It is like the laughter of a man or woman, who does not accept the alignment or the colour or the number or the size of his or her teeth. Such a person cannot laugh with the mouth open totally, but laughs with tightly closed lips. It is a complex. If you do not like your teeth do something about them. You can have false teeth. These days you can always have a thing without the thing being there. You can have coffee without coffee or milk without milk; you can walk without walking, row without rowing, cycle without cycling, without moving anywhere. You can hair without hair, you can have hair of any colour without that colour; you can have teeth without teeth, exactly as you want!

When you laugh tight-lipped there is a smile inside, but your complex of not wanting to show your teeth inhibits it. When you burst out laughing at a joke or whatever, at that moment you find the world is totally acceptable: your teeth are acceptable, your height is acceptable and more importantly, your weight is acceptable. Everything that you complain about is now acceptable to you, which means that you see yourself as totally acceptable and one who cannot be bettered.

It reveals a wholeness about you that is not opposed to the world. You do not shy away from the world. If you are afraid of the world you have a perennial problem, since the world is there wherever you go.

Once a Swami came to Rishikesh all the way from Kanyakumari, wanting a quiet place for meditation. I suggested a hut near the place where I was staying, but he chose a place beyond Rishikesh called Brahmapuri. It was a nice place on the banks of Ganga with facilities for *bhikṣā*, food in a temple nearby. There was nothing else around except trees. He had a very quiet life. After a month he came to me and said that he wanted to go to Uttarkasi. When I asked him:

"Why do you want to shift from Brahmapuri?"

"Swamiji, this place is noisy."

"How? Nobody is there."

"Swamiji, there are too many birds. All around me there are birds. In the morning I cannot meditate because they go on making noise."

I discouraged him from going to Uttarkasi as the place would be very cold during November. Nevertheless, he went and afterwards he never came back to Rishikesh. I made enquires and learnt that within fifteen days he had gone back to Kanyakumari—at least he was enlightened. The enlightenment is that wherever you go the world is with you. The problem is not the world; the problem is you.

Lord Kṛṣṇa in the *Bhagavad Gītā* gives us a wonderful advice. He says[5], "Keep all the external sense objects external." What an advice! The sense objects, that include everything that disturbs you, every being that bothers you from a mosquito onwards, are already external. Therefore, why should you keep them external? It is like saying 'keep the car outside' when it is already outside. One can accomplish only something that is possible. Suppose there is a mandate, "Do not drink fire or molten iron." Such a mandate is not valid because nobody drinks fire or molten iron when one is thirsty. If however, 'Do not drink alcohol' is a mandate, it can be followed because it is possible to drink alcohol. You can prohibit somebody from doing something only when there is such a possibility.

Therefore, when all the objects are external, why should Lord Kṛṣṇa ask us to keep them external? This is because some of them are not merely external, but are also internal. Anybody who bothers you is not only outside, but inside also. Even if the person is out of sight he is still inside because we carry a lot of load inside. To unload the people and to allow them to be what they are, definitely takes a certain understanding, a certain know-how. Most of the people are those who have hurt you at one time or the other, in one manner or the other. They become the objects of your frustration. In other words, you have an agenda for them. Your agenda for the other may be very noble, very reasonable and proper but the other person also has agenda for you. The main item in

---

[5] *sparśān kṛtvā bahir bāhyān* (*Bhagavad Gītā* 5.27).

his list is, 'Please drop your agenda for me.' This is his first agendum. Therefore, everybody has agenda for the other because people are not acceptable as they are. Consequently, you do not meet the person as he or she is. He or she is always a futuristic person in your thinking; that is, he should be this or she should be that to be acceptable. In spite of all this, I want you to understand that the implication of a moment of happiness is that the people inside your mind are kept outside. You find that all your frustrations get resolved. This is called wholeness.

The wholeness includes both the subject and the object

The wholeness is not against the world; it includes the world. The very world that you complain about is the world that does not pose a threat to you. You are the subject, the experiencer, and the object that is experienced. When you are the experiencer of your favourite melody in music, and you are happy listening to it, the object, the music that you experience, is able to completely swallow, devour all your complaints. In fact, it swallows the memory-based you, the wanting you. What remains is the objective 'you,' the appreciative 'you.' The subject, you, and the object, music, become one. This is what we call wholeness. The *dṛk*, subject, and the *dṛśya*, object, form one whole.

This wholeness is never lost. It is a reality. It cannot be completely relegated to the background just because you think in a particular way. The thinking itself is suspended, your will is suspended, your notion about yourself is suspended. In sleep you do suspend them, in a moment of happiness also you suspend them. This is a great blessing that we have. People look for the Lord's blessings. The greatest blessing, I say, is that you can suspend all your thinking, all your notions for the time being; otherwise it is not possible for anybody to be alive. Lord Kṛṣṇa says that forgetting, dropping all your ideas is the key to learning. That is how we learn. You may have well-entrenched ideas. You may have emotionally invested a lot in certain conclusions, about people and their opinions, about *gurus* etc. Later you do not want to give up those ideas, including those ideas that we can give up, in the wake of understanding. For the understanding to take place we should be able to keep all our ideas suspended for the time being and be alive to what we read or listen to now. That capacity is the basis for all learning. We have been given that capacity. That is the reason why if there is anything striking or inspiring, it devours the memory-based you, the wanting you, completely and you find there is wholeness.

Happiness is your nature

Our *śāstra* says that the wholeness is exactly what you are. There should not be, need not be, any reason whatsoever for you to be happy. You are happy without any reason, which means you are *unmatta,* abnormal. There are two types of people who are considered abnormal: people who are depressed or hilarious all the time and people who are wise. The hilarious one will stand in the middle of the road and suddenly laugh. You do not know the reason for his laughter, for he lives in his own world. A wise person has a semblance to the hilarious person. In fact, a wise person sees something within and he laughs, but externally there is no reason. A sugar crystal is sweet because it cannot be otherwise, whereas there is a reason if the water inside the pot is hot. There you can ask a question and get an answer.

"Why is the water hot?"

"Because the pot is hot."

"Why is the pot hot?"

"Because the pot is sitting on a hot plate."

"Why is the plate hot?"

"Because it is sitting on fire."

"Why is the fire hot?"

"But there is no cold fire."

There can be a scientific answer for the heat in the fire, but that does not change the fact that the fire is hot. Fire is hot. Similarly, one is happy for no reason. There is no answer to the question: "Why is a wise person happy?"

Being happy is not a matter for complaint for anybody. That is why when somebody is happy you do not sympathise with that person and enquire, "Why you, of all people, should be happy? You are such a great benefactor and a good person and therefore you should not be happy at all." Nor does anybody come to me and complain, "Swamiji, I do not know what is happening to me these days, I am very happy." Sometimes when you are very happy you become apprehensive that something untoward is going to happen. Otherwise, nobody complains about being happy and nobody enjoys being unhappy either. So the unhappy person is always consoled and sympathised with, because that is not natural to him or her. What is natural is not a matter for complaint.

You do not go to an ophthalmologist and ask him, "Doctor, please do something for me."

"What?"

"My eyes see."

The doctor, a kind man, and patient to this patient asked:

"Oh, do they see two where there is one?"

"No, no. I see one as one and two as two."

"Oh, are you not able to see objects very near?"

"No doctor, I can see, I can read."

"Oh, are you not able to see things far away?"

"No, I can see and read things far away too."

"Oh, are you not able to see in the evening?"

"No doctor, I see very well in the evening."

"Oh, then are you not able to see colours?"

"No, I can see all the colours. I see you are wearing a blue shirt."

"Then what is your problem?"

"I told you doctor in the beginning itself. My problem is that my eyes see."

The doctor said, "I see!" Being a kind person, he recommended that the person consult a specialist on the floor above.

Eyes are supposed to see. Ears are supposed to hear. You cannot say, "I ate in the morning and I am hungry again. I eat and I become hungry again. Therefore, there is something wrong with my stomach." Everything is all right with your stomach. If you are not hungry at all or always hungry, then that is a problem. Somebody complains, "Swamiji, I have too many desires." It means you are healthy. Your problem is not in having many desires. You do not know how to manage them; that is the problem. It is a management of riches. We do not know how to manage our riches.

So what is natural is not a matter for complaint. That you do not complain about being happy itself shows that it is natural for you to be happy. If it is natural to be happy, then why are you unhappy? It is very clear that you have a distorted view of yourself. The truth about you is totally different.

The 'I' is unique

There is no one like you. Not only is no one like you, there is nothing like you. First, let us understand the implications of this statement. In English, like in other languages, you have pronouns such as he, she, it, they and so on. A pronoun can stand for any noun including a dog. One can use the word 'it' for any neuter object and for any number of objects. The pronouns—he, she, and you—can refer to people, and the pronoun 'it' can refer to things. 'I' also is a pronoun. However, how many people are there for whom you can use 'I?' There is only one referent of 'I.' There is no second 'I' in the world. Do you know why? It is because there is only one 'I' and everything else is an object of that 'I.' One is 'I' and everything else is what becomes evident to that 'I.' There is nothing similar to this 'I.' It is just amazing.

All your complexes are born of comparison. You compare yourself with the similar and develop a complex. You can never compare yourself with the unlike and then develop a complex. Suppose there is a great western classical musician. He is jealous of a particular rock star, because when this rock star performs, his concert attracts millions; but when the classical musician gives a concert there are hardly twenty-five people, generally old, but who can understand his music. This makes the classical musician angry and jealous. The same classical musician will not sit by the wayside rock and lament, "Oh, rock, you are at peace with yourself whether it is sun or rain; you do not care whether somebody sits on you or spits on you; you are so at home. Whereas, at home, I am not at home; neither am I at home, outside. In fact, I am not at home with myself. I am jealous of you, oh, rock." He is, however, jealous of the rock star. Do you know why? A complex is always born of comparison, comparison with the like.

There is no other person, significant or insignificant from the standpoint of 'I.' The 'I' is unique. Everything else is evident to the 'I.' Our *śāstra* tells us very clearly that there are two facts one has to recognise. One is 'I-*ātman*-the seer,' and the other is 'not I-*anātman*-the seen.' There is no third factor. One may ask, "What about heaven?" Either heaven is 'you' or it is 'not you.' If heaven is you, then you have to understand what that heaven is. If it is not you, then definitely it is other than you. It comes under 'not I.'

Then what about God? If God is 'I' then he is five feet nine inches. If God is other than 'I' he also comes under 'not I.' Is God 'I' then? What is the implication? Maybe, God is both 'I' and 'not I.' Maybe everything is God. That is a possibility.

It is very clear that I am the subject and everything else is the object. This means that you cannot compare yourself with anybody. Therefore, when you say that a person is successful, it is a statement that reveals a judgement. People are judgemental. Those who are judgemental, I say, are mental. We even make God judgemental. People say that after death there is a judgement day. God will ask who you are and send you to hell if he does not approve of your name. He will choose those who will go to heaven. God is made into a judgemental person. I thought that God, at least, is free from being judgemental and is someone in whom I can seek refuge, someone who, in his wisdom, can accommodate me. He can look at my background and then say, "It is because of a background you are like this;

in fact, you are as good as anybody else." At least that is what he is supposed to say. Every therapist is able to say that. We do not need a judgemental God.

There is nothing wrong in one's concept of God. One is free to have and practice his or her set of beliefs. However, one cannot go about converting another person. This is violence because the aggressive religion thinks there is a rich harvest for conversion available and therefore it has to plant the cross in Asia. Are you a crop to be harvested? A harvest means a wholesale harvesting by conversion.

In spite of this person committing the sin of calling you a sinner, is not a sinner in the vision of our *śāstra*. That is India and her culture. We have to be aware of our riches, our culture. In spite of these onslaughts, India still survives. We survive, in spite of the politicians, in spite of our callous attitude towards our tradition, our culture, our religion, and our spirituality.

'I' is self-evident awareness

Our *śāstra* says that you are unlike everything else. Everything in this world is evident to you. You see a flower in the garden; it is evident to you. A thing exists because it comes to your knowledge, through a means of knowledge. The sun, the moon and the stars are, because they are evident to you. Black holes are; they are evident to you through inference. That he is or she is, is evident to you. Your body is; it is evident to you. Your eyes see; it is evident to you. They do not see; it is also evident to you. You have this particular thought at this moment; it is evident to you. You have, in your memory, your experience of Delhi; that is evident to you. That it is not in your memory is also evident to you. What you know, the knowledge is evident to you. What you do not know, the ignorance is evident to you.

Everything becomes evident to you; 'you' also means 'I.' Now I will ask you a question, "Do you exist or not?" What will you say? You cannot say that you will consult someone and let me know. When you say 'I am' it means 'I exist.' The 'am' is a verb of being. 'I am' means 'I is.'

To whom is 'I am' evident? If everything is evident to you then are you not there? "Yes, I am." To whom is the existence of the self, evident? The self is evident to the self. In other words you are self-evident. Everything else is evident to you and therefore you are unlike everything else. Everything becomes evident to you, no matter what exists, how far it exists, how great it is, how big it is.

In Sanskrit there are these two words, *bhāti,* meaning shines and *anubhāti,* meaning shines after. We have to know these two words very well. *Anu* is a prefix whose literal meaning is 'after.' When you say that a thing exists, it exists because you happen to know it. The objects in the world do not have a capacity to reveal themselves without your knowing them through the appropriate means of knowledge.

You have eyes that are capable of sight. Your eyes cannot perceive anything without picking up the light.

Sight is always in terms of picking up the light. You see your physical body. It does not shine on its own. It is lighted. Therefore, the physical body shines after, whereas the light shines. All opaque objects are not self-radiant and are picked up by our eyes, in terms of reflected light.

The sources of light like fire, the sun, the stars, a lamp and even a glow-worm are self-luminous, but they also shine after, *anubhāti*. How? The light in your eyes lights up the sun. It is a light of perception, of awareness. The light in your eyes is the light of awareness because of which you are aware of the sun, moon, stars and so on. All objects, including all sources of light, shine because the eyes shine. The eyes shine because the mind, behind the eyes, shines. The mind shines because the 'I' is behind the mind. The 'I' shines because I am self-evident, self-luminous. The shine here is the light. What kind of a light? It is the light by which you see lights. It is the light because of which everything comes to light. This is 'you.' The Self-luminous 'you' is the one to be understood. When you recognise this fact, then that is the ultimate success. When you understand the self-evident 'you', you are freeing yourself from being judgemental.

Talk 5

You Are Self-Evident

You are a singular person. This is not merely by your unique individuality, but because of the very profound fact that you are the only person who is self-evident while everything else becomes evident to you. Anything you objectify is evident to you including time and space, either by direct perception or inference. Whether the object is macro or micro, it becomes evident to you. Your own body is no exception; it is evident to you. Lord Kṛṣṇa in the *Bhagavad Gītā* says[6] that this body is a *kṣetra*. *Kṣetra* means a field of experience, an object of experience, an object of knowledge. Even though you identify your physical body as 'I', Lord Kṛṣṇa says that it is an object of the pronoun 'this' because you are able to objectify every part of your body as 'this.' Therefore, your body is a *kṣetra*. The only one who is self-evident, is the one for whom everything else is evident. In every piece of evidence, what is present is consciousness.

'I' the consciousness is limitless

I can put it differently for better understanding. When you say that the Swami is, Swami consciousness is. The sun is, the sun consciousness is. Space is, space consciousness is. Time is, time consciousness is.

[6] *idaṁ śarīraṁ kaunteya kṣetram ityabhidhīyate* (*Bhagavad Gītā* 13.1).

Your body is, body consciousness is. A given thought or emotion is, that emotion consciousness is. Memory is, memory consciousness is. Ignorance is, ignorance consciousness is. I am, I consciousness is. Therefore, consciousness is always present and is unlike everything else, because everything else is an object of consciousness.

This consciousness does not have any particular form or size. Suppose I ask you, "What is the distance between these two hands?" You can guess that the distance is, more or less, two feet. If I ask, "What is the distance between the hand and the space?" Any distance is between two points in space. Between a point in space and space, there is no point in asking 'What is the distance?' There is no distance. Space, being all-pervasive, is in and through my hand. Therefore, between a point in space and space the distance is zero; between space and stars there is no distance; between space and your body there is no distance; but between your body on this earth and the stars there is a distance, a distance of light years, because they are two points in space. Between your body and my body there is a distance.

Now, what is the distance between consciousness and the body? If you say space, then what is the distance between space and consciousness? There is no distance. Space is consciousness. Time is consciousness. But consciousness is not space or time. This is the most important fact. It means that consciousness is not located in a place. Consciousness has no height. It has no width. All that is there is one spatially limitless consciousness.

It is this limitless whole that you experience whenever you are happy. Neither the subject nor the object is away from consciousness nor do they stand opposed to consciousness. They are sustained by this consciousness, which is the meaning of the word 'I.' What is, is nothing but consciousness, which is both the subject and the object. This wholeness is you. Our *śāstra* goes further to point out that you are not only spatially limitless, but you are also time-wise limitless. Time is not going to bind you anymore, for you swallow time and survive time. Time is, time-consciousness is. When you are in deep sleep, time disappears; when time is not, consciousness still is.

The truth of time is consciousness

The concept of time, whether subjective or objective, is not always the same; from time to time, the time series keeps on changing. Einstein once said that if you want to understand the relative nature of time, all that you have to do is stand on a hot plate, barefoot, for a minute. You will find every second excruciatingly long. However, when a person talks to his or her beloved, then he or she finds that time develops wings. This is the relative nature of time. It either hangs on you or it just disappears; well, it all depends upon what it is that you are engaged in. This is subjective time.

There is an objective time related to the speed of light, which is 184000 miles per second. We measure the speed of everything else only in relation to this. There is no absolute time, truly speaking. Whether time is subjective or objective, it is not away from consciousness.

If this is so, then do you experience time in sleep? No. In sleep, time disappears, space disappears, your knowledge disappears; everything disappears. All differences are resolved; a beggar is no longer a beggar. Similarly there is no royal sleep when a king goes to sleep. The scholar is no longer a scholar, the ignorant no longer ignorant. Sleep is a levelling experience. The kings, the citizens, the rich, the poor, the elite, all of them are levelled in sleep. In fact, all are the same as long as they are asleep. You can only say that everyone is as good as everyone else in sleep. All that is there is the experience of 'I do not know anything.' Your individuality disappears, but you, the basic person, consciousness, does not disappear. That is why, getting up in the morning, you can say, "I slept well." You are very much there in sleep.

In sleep you are not aware of time and place, whereas in the dream there is time. You create time in the dream. In deep sleep you are there, minus time. The consciousness, being not bound by space or time, is limitlessness, which is the *ātman*, the 'I.' Timelessness is always in the form of 'now', the present moment. If you look at what is 'now', it is going to be timelessness alone. There is a beautiful verse:[7] "The past and the future were 'present' at their own time. Is not the concern about the past and future, without understanding the truth of the

---

[7] *bhūtaṁ bhaviṣyacca bhavat svakāle, tad varttamānasya vihāya tattvam, hāsyā na kiṁ syāt gata-bhāvi-carcā, vinaika saṅkhyāṁ gaṇaneva loke. (Sat Darśan* Verse 17*)*

present, a matter for laughter? It is similar to counting without knowing the numeral **one**."

When you think of time in terms of the past, or the future, one thing becomes very evident. The past was always present; the future will unfold itself as present. Then what is present? We can say a block of time is the present. How do you understand this block of time in terms of the present?

Let us analyse the truth of the present block of time. What is the length of time the present should have? If you say the present block of time is one year, then one year has twelve months. If the present is taken as one month, a month has four weeks. If you say one week is the present, then there are seven days in a week. If one day is considered as the present, a day has twenty-four hours. If the present block of time is one hour, sixty minutes make an hour. Maybe, the present block is one minute, but there are sixty seconds in a minute. Is one second the length of the present time? A second has one million microseconds. Can we say one micro second is the present? No. It has again one million pico seconds. Thanks to the progress in information technology, one can mathematically go on dividing further.

Then what is the present? Well, the present is consciousness that is aware of the disappearance of time. When you think of a length of time, time consciousness is there and when that length of time disappears, there is consciousness. This is the present. In fact, the presence of consciousness is the present. It is always whole, always limitless.

Therefore, will it not be a matter for laughter when you are so concerned about the past, and worried about the future without knowing the truth of the past and the future? The past was the present and the future will be the present. Therefore, understand what is the present. It is like a person who does not know what the value of 'one' is and yet wants to study calculus.

You are not subject to time, not subject to any spatial limitation, and therefore, you cannot say that you are affected by the world. In fact you sustain the whole world. You are already free. This is what they call *sat-cit-ānanda*. *Sat* means not bound by time; it is always present in all situations. *Cit* means consciousness and *ānanda* is the spatial limitlessness. This is the truth about you. This is the insight I want you to have. If this is you, then how can you say that you are not successful? Own up the truth first; nothing can be more than what is the whole.

What is non-negatable is satya

Somebody asked me, "Swamiji, you have been saying that 'I am the whole' and the Upaniṣads also say the same. Suppose a modern philosopher proves that I am more than the whole. What will I do?" I said to him, "What cannot be bettered is the whole; what cannot be negated is *satya*."

Once, I was addressing the faculty members in a university campus. One of them was a physicist who was listening to my talks. I had about four or five talks. In the first talk I said, "Vedanta is a means of knowledge to reveal the truth of yourself, truth of the world."

Then, at the end of that talk, this physicist came to me and asked:

" Swami, may I ask a question?"

"Yes."

"Did you say Vedanta reveals the truth?"

"Yes."

"Is not Vedanta words?"

"Yes."

"Do you say the words reveal the truth?"

"Yes."

"How can words reveal the truth?"

"Why should they not?"

"No, words are limited."

"I know they are limited. In fact, I can talk much more about the limitations of words. In spite of knowing the limitations very well, I say the words reveal the truth."

"So you are going to define the truth."

"Yes, I am going to define the truth."

"If you can define the truth, then every definition is from a point of view."

"That may be true. But I have my own definitions."

"Then, tell me, how."

"I will tell you tomorrow, please come to the lecture."

He wanted it just then. He said, "Swami I am coming to the lecture tomorrow, but please tell me right now. How are you going to define truth?"

I said, "What cannot be negated is truth."

"What?"

"What can never be negated is truth."

"My God, that is a very big definition."

The physicist went back, came the next day and before the talk asked me:

"Swami, this is an amazing definition, but then is there such a thing? I cannot wait; I have to know now. I will come to your talk later, but please tell me now, is there such a thing?"

"Yes, there is such a truth."

"What is it?"

"It is you."

"Me?"

"Yes."

"How?"

"Try to negate yourself, come on. The one who goes about negating cannot be negated."

He said, "That is true, that is true!"

Afterwards, his problem was, "How come I did not know this?"

Consciousness cannot be negated; but you can negate everything else. You can dismiss anything from a different standpoint. You can say, "This is a disposable cup." You can also invert the same cup and negate it saying, "This is not a cup, but merely a form of plastic." There is no cup. It is gone. After inverting the cup, you cannot say that it is a cup and pour coffee into it.

You can define a thing from a point of view and dismiss the very same thing from another point of view. You can do this with all things. You cannot, however, dismiss the consciousness that you are. You are *satya*. You are what you really want to be.

To look upon yourself as a failure, is absolutely a judgement and that too a wrong one. Neither are you a failure nor is anyone else a failure. If this is the insight you have about yourself, everything else is a plus for you. At the level of consciousness itself you are complete, limitless, whole. Then the mind, which is an addition, is a luxury. That the mind can emote, can desire is a blessing. That you can have ambitions is a blessing. That you can will is another blessing. That you can explore and discover is a blessing. That there are other truthful people who are your contemporaries is a blessing. That you have a good memory, like a floppy, to store information and to be able to remember and recollect at the right time is yet another blessing.

When you are the whole, the limitless, where is the question of your feeling incomplete and lonely? The loneliness that you feel is not because you have no people around. In fact, there are too many people around, but still you feel lonely. Do you know why? It is because you feel that others do not understand you. It has nothing to do with the others; it has everything to do with only you. You feel that you are not understood. Why do you not understand others? Seeing yourself as a person who is empty inside there is a sense of want, a sense of inadequacy. You want to break that sense of inadequacy and therefore you seek understanding from others.

The wholeness cannot be improved

You have to see yourself in the light of the *śāstra,* wherein you cannot be made better. Nobody can improve the whole or make it better. You are the whole and nobody can change that. That is the greatness of our *śāstra,* for it has the truth. We have the last word; no one can improve this, not even the Lord.

If a new theology arises it will say only something less, and that is, 'You are not the whole.' You miss what is evident and then study all these theologies. What is your conclusion after seriously studying these theologies? You come to the very same conclusion that you are not the whole. Even without serious study, long before entering the study of theology, your conclusion was that the world is different from you. Therefore, no theology is going to improve this vision: You are the whole, *pūrṇa*. The word *puruṣa* itself reveals that meaning. *Puruṣa* means the indweller of this body.[8] The one who indwells is you,

---

[8] *purau uṣati iti puruṣaḥ.*

the individual. Again, the one who fills up everything[9] is *puruṣa*. The word *ātman* also has the same meaning. *Āpnoti sarvam iti ātmā*, the one who pervades everything is the *ātman*. What more do you want? Our *ṛṣis*, seers, have given us the heritage. They have given it not just to us, but also to the entire humanity. It is too ancient even to claim that it is Indian.

No knowledge can be considered as Indian, American or Argentinean. Knowledge is knowledge for everybody, whether it is simple arithmetic of one plus one or the profound truth that you are the limitless. The advantage we have in India is that we have a tradition of teaching. Unfortunately, it is not available elsewhere in the world. Though there may be people conveying the same thing, there is no tradition of teaching. Thanks to our *ācāryas*, our masters, who spent and committed their lives for this and held it together, we have the vision; the tradition of teaching is still available today. If I am able to communicate this vision to you, it is nothing but the grace of all these great masters, their efforts to retain this against all odds. It has to be preserved.

Suppose, the Egyptian government comes up with a new housing scheme. It decides to retain just one pyramid and knock off all the other pyramids and use the stones for building houses under this big housing scheme. Do you think that humanity will let it happen? Never. That sacrilege will never be allowed to happen. Do you know why? It is because the pyramids are not

---

[9] *pūrṇatvāt puruṣaḥ*.

Egyptian anymore. They belong to the human genius. It is a standing, colossal monument of the human genius. Even though the culture that built them was destroyed totally, they stand there as a monument of human genius; they are not Egyptian anymore. Egypt has the privilege only to protect them.

Similarly, this tradition of communicating the vision that you are the whole is a blessing to humanity. It is the treasure of humanity. It is also very ancient; we should not allow it to be destroyed by a papal intervention and a programme of conversion. There is nothing emotional here. I am absolutely clear about what I am saying. I love freedom for all people. Every person has the freedom to practice his or her religion; but the freedom to practice is not a sanction for the elimination of other religions. A programme of conversion goes in that direction. It is wrong. Every culture should be preserved for there is something unique in every culture. It will be a misfortune to miss that culture. If humanity has something as the last word in human endeavour, in human accomplishment, something that is ultimate, this is it. You are the whole. Nobody can improve it.

What cannot be negated is *satya* and that is what we are talking about. It is neither bound by time nor space; it has neither a beginning nor an end. When you say, "I am *sat-cit-ānanda*," they are not words for you; the words are you. And what is more, that *satya* is what you are and it cannot be bettered. Therefore, you cannot be more successful than what you are already. Until you discover that, the journey continues.

TALK 6

Relative Success Through Yoga

As self-conscious beings, we have complexes that we are small, we are limited, and so on. These complexes prevent us from accepting the truth of ourselves. If the truth of your self is intimately understood, you have made it. You cannot say, "I am not qualified." What can deny you this knowledge? For what are you not qualified? Is it mountaineering? It is neither mountaineering nor learning calculus. It is just seeing what you are. Nothing disqualifies you; but if you find that there is some problem in seeing this, then it is worthwhile resolving it. That is what life is about. You can be very successful only if you completely resolve all the inhibiting factors.

Managing one's desires

Relatively speaking, success does not mean fulfilling all your desires because it is a fact that you cannot fulfil them. As we have already seen, no human being has fulfilled all his or her desires. Everybody has unfulfilled desires. Therefore, there is no way you can become successful by fulfilling all your desires. Then, what is the way? Perhaps there is relative success when you know how to manage your desires. Desires are a manifestation of a privilege that you have. The cow does not have the capacity to desire a video camera. You have this capacity. So, you look at this desire as a privilege.

Desire is not a problem. People who are supposed to enlighten you create a complex in you when they say, "Desires create problems and therefore do not have desires. If you do not have desires, you will have no disappointments, no blood pressure problem." Then there is a workshop that says, "You should be free from desires. If all desires dry up in you, you will realise yourself." You attend this workshop and now, you have a new desire that from now on you should give up all your desires. You also develop a new complex. Previously, you could not fulfil all your desires and therefore you were a failure. Now, you cannot give up this new desire and therefore you are a worse failure. These people encash everything, including your breathing. They will advise you to breathe this way and breathe that way and call it a special way of living. You have to review all this.

In fact, desires are a manifestation of Īśvara and hence, desiring itself is not a problem. It is the lack of understanding the whole dynamic of desiring, desires and their fulfilments that needs to be addressed. The more you understand, the better you are at handling and managing your desires.

Basically, you are a cognitive person. Even the person who argues, "Swamiji, I am emotional," is also cognitive. He may say, "Swamiji, I do not like too much thinking, too much reasoning because reasoning makes me tired." Reasoning does not make one tired; it is wrong reasoning that makes one tired. When the person argues, there is no emotion in his argument. It is only when he loses the argument that he becomes emotional. Therefore, basically one is cognitive. When one studies psychology, it is all cognitive. Any therapy ends in a cognitive situation. You have to resolve a lot of things by changing cognitively. In other words, you have to understand the 'whole.'

Hinduism is a view and way of life

The *Gītā* gives us a way of life. Once, our Late President, Dr. Radhakrishnan, was asked by somebody, "How will you define Hinduism?" He said, "It is a view and a way of life." You cannot say it better. It is a view of life and the way is to accomplish that view. The view is that you are the whole. You are not a sinner. You are not born of any imperfection. You are not born of somebody's criminal action of going against God. You are born within the order of Īśvara. This means that you can see that you are the whole. This is the last and the ultimate message.

In India also, there are different theologies, different schools of thought such as *dvaita*, dualism, *viśiṣṭādvaita*, qualified non-dualism, and so on. You name any theology in the world; we have it here. Even though they are theologies, one good thing about them is that they do not cause any problem because they do not have the 'saviour' concept. Nobody interferes in your relating to Īśvara, because of the basic vision. The view of life is that you are the whole, and the whole way of life is meant to help you understand that view. That is why the way of life in our society was designed for this. It was a society with no competition. By profession, the son of a goldsmith was a goldsmith and the son of a blacksmith was a blacksmith. So, there was no competition.

Nowadays, because the child has to compete, the child is pushed so much that he or she cannot have a childhood. This is not our society. We did not bargain for this. Our forefathers, I think, were much safer. They had the leisure to sing and listen to music. They produced classical literature and so on. However, it is different today. For instance, a father wants his teenage son to learn classical music. The son has different ideas. Not only must his music come from abroad, he must also have a music hero. The father wants him to have an exposure to Indian classical music and takes him to a concert. Within a few minutes the boy looks at his watch because he cannot handle slow music. He cannot sing or listen to music; he only knows to do music. Today, there is no leisure and there is nothing classical. The only classic we have is the Coke Classic. Thanks to the Coca Cola Company, because of them we have something classic!

I do not say that the society that was there before was right or wrong. All I can say, definitely, is that there was no competition in the society and a child had his or her childhood. When there is no childhood, what is progress and where is the structure in a society?

The earlier society had a structure. In this well-defined structure, even a mediocre person would pass because excellence was only in one's growth as a person. One excelled in whichever field he or she chose, whether it was the Vedas or the auxiliaries of the Vedas, like grammar and prosody, or it was music or art. There was growth because there was something to accomplish.

It was a perfect structure for a spiritual goal. That is why Dr. Radhakrishnan said that Hinduism is a view and a way of life.

Even now, the view of life has not changed but the way of life has definitely changed. There is nothing wrong in the change, if one has a certain inner strength to face all these competitions. Therefore, it is important that you understand the way of life, which is called *yoga* in the *Bhagavad Gītā*. It is much more necessary now; otherwise we cannot make it. Everybody has to know this. The entire humanity has to know. It is a question of understanding and in the wake of understanding there are certain attitudes, which are consequential, which will bless you.

The way you live your life should be such that it helps you discover yourself. To be in touch with yourself is to be in touch with the whole. You also know that you cannot meet with success in life by fulfilling all your desires. There is only one way that is open to you. You have to learn to be on top of your desires.

The desires can be looked at from two different standpoints. One is the desire to acquire, to possess, to own, to experience and to accomplish what you do not have. There is also the desire to retain what you already have, your money, your health, your youthfulness, your current weight, a relationship and so on. All these consume your time and energy. They all demand action on your part. Lord Kṛṣṇa calls these desires *ragas*, likes.

The second type, the opposite is an equally powerful desire. This is the desire to avoid what you do not want.

You want to avoid illness, old age, loss of money, loss of face, loss of power and so on. You also want to avoid certain people. In fact, this type of desire is also equally time consuming and action demanding. Lord Kṛṣṇa calls these *dveṣa*s, dislike.

Therefore, one is *rāga,* to acquire what you want, retain what you have and the other is *dveṣa,* to avoid, get rid of what you do not want. You do not court a headache, but you experience it. You do not court any illness, but you do fall ill. There are a lot of things that sneak into your life, which you want to get rid off. Sometimes, you want to get hold of something and with great enthusiasm you pursue and get it. Soon it becomes a thing that you want to get rid of. What you wanted earlier, you do not want any more, or what you did not want earlier, you want now. Thus, *rāga-dveṣa*s sometimes jump from one category to the other. They are variable. They are neither good nor bad; they are there.

Human life is lived, dictated and driven by one's own likes and dislikes. There is nothing wrong in it. Even Lord Kṛṣṇa had his own likes; he loved to play the flute, he loved to dance. He had his own style of standing; he always stood stylishly with three bends, the *tribhaṅga,* and he loved to adorn his head with a peacock feather.

The way of life taught by the Gitā

Your likes and dislikes are not really a problem. The problem arises only when they decide when you should be happy or unhappy. A lack of mastery over your *rāga*s and *dveṣa*s keeps you under their control. They dictate your life and tyrannise you. They are no longer privileges.

If a privilege becomes a curse, you have to restore that privilege. In order to do this, you must have a certain space to look at your likes and dislikes. You should be able to choose and have the upper hand. In other words you have to be a 'swami.' Everyone has to become a swami. Swami means the one who is in charge of his or her life. To be a swami or a swamini is to manage these likes and dislikes for which Lord Kṛṣṇa gives us a whole plan of living as well as an insight into fulfilling this plan through *yoga*.

One of the definitions of *yoga* in the *Bhagavad Gītā* is '*yogaḥ karmasu kauśalam*,'[10] generally translated as 'skill in action is *yoga*.' By this definition, even a pickpocket or a clever criminal is a *yogin* because he is very skilful in action. In fact, Indian women are all *yogini*s in the kitchen, because they watch the movie on the television and cook at the same time. It is great skill in action.

Diligent practice of any activity can make you skilful. It is obvious then that skill is not *yoga*. It has nothing to do with *karma-yoga*. *Kauśala* is an important word in the definition to understand *karma-yoga*. Kṛṣṇa further defines *yoga* with reference to the results of action. "*...samatvaṁ yoga ucyate*."[11] *Yoga* is defined as evenness of mind. So *samatva* and *kauśala* are the defining words for *karma-yoga*.

---

[10] Chapter 2 Verse 50.
[11] Chapter 2 Verse 48.

A life of *karma-yoga* is meant to make you a swami, a master of your likes and dislikes. Whatever little knowledge you have about yourself, about the world, about actions and results, about your concept of success, well, it has only created problems for you. The *Gītā* presents a different vision about actions and results in the second chapter to help you manage your likes and dislikes and become a swami.

There are sentences in the *śāstra* that are *siddha-vastu viṣaya,* that are statements of fact, such as, the fire is hot or Indra has a thunderbolt in his hand. There are also sentences that prompt you to act or request you to do something. Let us look at this sentence in the second chapter of the *Gītā*:[12] "*karmaṇyevādhikāraste mā phaleṣu kadācana*...you have a choice only with reference to action, but definitely not with reference to the results of action." This is a statement of fact and not a piece of advice. Lord Kṛṣṇa does not say here, "Perform action, but do not expect results." Who will perform any action without expecting a result? I get this question all over the country, and it has travelled outside India too! "Swamiji, how can I perform action without expecting any result. That is difficult." I tell them, "It is not just difficult, it is foolish, please understand."

There is nobody who has performed an action without expecting a result. Even an involuntary action like breathing, closing and opening of our eyelids and so on produces a result. If involuntary actions produce results,

---

[12] Verse 47.

then voluntary actions definitely produce results. My communicating to you is meant to produce a result, the result of being understood by you. Lord Kṛṣṇa taught Arjuna, because he expected Arjuna to understand his teaching. Therefore, it is wrong to say, 'Perform action without expecting results.' If you say that the *Gītā* teaches this, then either the *Gītā* is wrong or you have misunderstood the teaching. If you dismiss the *Gītā* as wrong, then you have no *śraddhā,* but if you look into your understanding, then that is called *śraddhā.*

Let us look into what the *Gītā* says. In action alone there is a choice, but definitely not with reference to its result. It is not asking you to act without expecting a result. So both the prevalent definitions, namely, 'skill in action is *yoga*' and 'perform action without expecting a result' are wrong.

One has choice only with reference to one's action

The *Gītā* states a fact—that you have a choice over your action. This choice is not there for animals. A donkey, for instance, is not going to deliberate on whether it should kick this person or not. Animals do not have a choice over an action. They are free to act, but they are not free enough not to act. They are programmed to behave in a certain manner, whereas as a human being, even if you feel like kicking you can stop yourself. The capacity to refrain from an action, impulsive or otherwise, makes you a singular person among the living organisms on this planet. You have this privilege, which is freedom of choice over your action.

Since you have the privilege of choice, you have to decide what is proper and improper in your interaction with the world in terms of any action. All considerations come into the picture because what you do should not hurt others.

One has no choice over the results of action

Once you perform an action, the result is taken care of. Taken care of by what? Well, the results are controlled by the natural laws. In fact, the whole *jagat* is nothing but equations and laws. For instance, you have a choice to bring both the hands together to clap. Up to this point, the freedom is literally in your hands. However, once you choose to clap and you do clap, then the result is already predetermined and inevitable. If you want to clap and at the same time avoid the sound, then you have to bring the hands together differently. If you want to avoid the sound, just join the hands together to say *namaste*. However, if you bring the hands together by clapping, the laws, which are the order, take care of the result. You cannot avoid the resulting sound being produced. You realise that there is something wrong, because what you want is one thing, but what you do produces quite another. You have to learn from experience.

Your knowledge is very limited. When you perform an action, you expect certain results. However, there are many hidden variables that influence the outcome of your action. When you cannot control even the known variables, how can you control the hidden variables?

A number of laws, including the law of *karma*, are involved in determining the nature of the result.

If that is so, you have to understand very clearly that you can only plan and execute your action. You have to plan; you cannot dart into darkness. That is why the *buddhi*, the thinking faculty, is given. Once you have executed your plan you have to be ready to accept the outcome. This is called *samatva*, evenness of mind, with reference to both success and failure.

The result of an action has only four possibilities

For instance, you want to cross the road and catch the bus to reach home. There is nothing wrong in your desire. It is what everybody does. You want to ensure that you cross the road safely. Therefore, you do not just dart across, but do your homework. You look on either side, cross the road and catch the bus. Nevertheless, things do not happen always as you plan. There are four possible results for your action. You cross the road and catch the bus, which often happens. Sometimes, you cross the road and miss the bus. You cross the road and get a ride, a rare possibility. The fourth option is that you were crossing the road. Two days later you wake up in the nearest local hospital, and ask some fundamental questions such as "Who am I?" (laughter).

The four possibilities can be stated differently. It can be equal to your expectation, that is, crossing the road and catching the bus. It could be less than your expectation, which is, missing the bus. It could also be more than your expectation, which is getting a ride. It could be just the opposite of your expectation; you did not even cross the road.

So, Lord Kṛṣṇa says that you do not have any choice over the results of your action. The results are taken care of by the laws that also include the law of *karma*. The law of *karma* sometimes works in your favour and sometimes against. Many of you have experienced this. When the stocks were going up, you thought that you would buy some stocks. The day you bought the stocks, they went down. Then you wanted to sell them, so that you could get back some money. The day you sold them, the stocks went up. What does it mean? It only means that you do not produce the results of action; it is the law of *karma* that produces the results.

This is where *karma-yoga* begins. You perform an action to achieve a desired result. You plan, you organise, you do your homework. That is the correct thing to do. Subsequently, the expected results may or may not happen. You learn from your experience. You need to have a certain attitude born of understanding. This attitude forms a part of *karma-yoga*. The understanding here is that it is given to you to act, while the result is taken care of by the laws, by the order of Īśvara. Īśvara is not only the Lord of the laws, of the order; he is the order. Lord Kṛṣṇa says,[13] "a human being gains success by

---

[13] *yataḥ pravṛttirbhūtānaṁ yena sarvam idaṁ tatam, svakarmaṇā tam abhyarcya siddhiṁ vindati mānavaḥ* (*Bhagavad Gītā* 18.46).

worshipping him from whom everything has come, by whom all these are pervaded, through the performance of one's duty." This verse is meant to convert our entire life into *yoga*. It has to be thoroughly understood for successful living.

Īśvara is the maker and the material

Now, is there a Lord? Is there a creation? The word creation is a red rag for every physicist, every scientist and every biologist. This is because, for them the *jagat,* the universe is a manifestation. It is amazing how a scientist is able to see even the stages of manifestation and present how the universe was twelve billion years ago, long before it came about. Therefore, for him, it is only a manifestation and not a creation at all.

Our *śāstra* supports the scientists' view of the universe that everything is a manifestation. Your eyes are particles, as are your ears. Wherever there is a cell, there are molecules and atoms in the molecules. There are particles in the atoms. Can the particles be intelligent enough to become your eyes, your ears, to become the right and left side of the brain? Do you think they assemble themselves intelligently? Or are they in the hands of someone intelligent?

This is where 'Theo' God comes, because without knowledge all things being 'intelligently put together' is not possible. The word 'all,' *sarva,* means things that you know and do not know. There is no other 'all.' So this 'intelligently putting together' presupposes all knowledge and knowledge cannot rest anywhere, except in a conscious being. There must be an all-knowing, conscious being, without which there is no possibility of anything being intelligently put together.

Every theology in the world has a concept of God. Where is this God, the all-knowing, conscious being? What is his location? They say that God in heaven created the world. A child can ask his father:

"Dad, who made this sun?"

"God."

"Where is this God?"

"In heaven."

"Where is this heaven?"

"Up above."

"Dad, did you ever go there?"

"Not yet."

"Can we go now, dad?"

"No, not now, later we will go, do not worry."

"Dad, did God in heaven create this world?"

"Yes."

"Dad, who created heaven?"

"God."

"Oh! God created heaven?"

"Yes."

"Dad, where was God before he created heaven?"

"Shut up. Do not ask silly questions."

The boy has not yet lost his innocence, his questioning mind. He thinks for a while and comes up with an answer that seems logical for him.

"Dad, I know where was God before he created heaven."

"Where was he?"

"Dad, you said there is one more place called hell. So, God in hell created the heaven."

Poor dad said, "That is true, it looks like that."

The boy did not stop with this:

"Dad, tell me who created hell?"

"God created hell."

"Why did he create a hell for himself?"

"Because he made a mistake."

"Dad, does God also commit mistakes?"

"He committed a mistake just once."

Therefore, these questions—who created heaven and hell, where was God before he created heaven, what was the material he used—beg for an answer and they will beg forever. Nobody is going to answer these questions; they cannot. The theology itself has to fold up because it has no answer. All the theologies believe that God sits somewhere above and watches you all the time; this is precisely what the scientists are against.

You could, however, frame the question differently. Instead of asking, "Where is God?" you can ask, "What is God?" You need not conclude that God needs a location. Since both space and time are part of the whole setup, the *jagat*, God cannot be within space and create space. Your car is outside and you are inside, but both the car and you are within space. What does outside space or inside space mean? There is only space. Where is the question of God being inside or outside space? There is, however, one other possibility, a third possibility, which is, perhaps space itself is not separate from God. That is a great possibility.

Once we have understood the concept of space not being separate from God, we need to look into the question of the material. With what did God create this world? Where did he find the material? You cannot say that he created out of nothing. One can argue that God can do anything, but can one assimilate it? Space and time, as we have seen, are a part of the creation. So, the only possibility is that the maker is not separate from the material. There is no other possibility.

If you talk of creation, then it implies a maker, a creator, who must necessarily be all knowledge and all power. It is easy for the human mind to appreciate an efficient cause, a maker, who has all the knowledge and all the power to make whatever is here. Further, creation also implies material that cannot be different from that maker.

Let us look at this example. A pot-maker creates a pot out of clay, the material. The clay is separate from the pot-maker. When you buy a pot, the pot-maker does not come along. If he did, then you would not buy anything. Such things, however, do not happen because the maker is different from the material. Between the pot-maker and the material, clay, there is space, where there is neither the clay nor the pot-maker. This is very important for separation. With reference to the all-knowledge, intelligent being, however, it is different. If there is a separation between the maker, the all-intelligent, conscious being and the material, that gap has to be established by space; and space itself is a manifestation. Therefore, the material cause and the maker cannot be separate.

So, although the pot-maker is separate from the pot, between the product and the material there is no separation. The material is where the product is. For instance, you cannot have a shirt without the material. You cannot even imagine a shirt minus its material. The shirt is the material. In short, you cannot have anything without the material that sustains it.

The logic that the maker and the material are separate is not applicable to the total creation. The logic that is available for something within the total is not applicable to the total. In mathematics, you know that one plus one is two. Yet, when you think of infinity, infinity plus one or one million, is still infinity. Infinity plus infinity is infinity, infinity minus infinity also is infinity. What cannot be improved upon is infinity. Therefore, the logic applicable to a finite quantity does not extend itself to cover infinity. Thus, when the *Gītā* says, "From the Lord everything has come, by the Lord everything is pervaded," it means that the material cause is not separate from that Lord. Therefore, all that is here is a manifestation.

The physicist is ecstatic when he hears me saying, "All that is here is a manifestation." This is what he looks for because he knows how the particles move methodically. Yet, the physicist has a problem to solve. He knows that the probability of anything not being there is equal to or greater than its being there. Particles have to turn at the right place and in the right way; otherwise you will have something else manifesting. The whole progression is gradual, methodical and intelligent, which means that it is a manifestation of knowledge, all knowledge. The maker and the material being identical makes the whole thing very alive, and the knowledge of this, is highly redeeming.

Talk 7

Every Form Is Īśvara

You can assimilate the vision of the maker and the material being identical by using the dream world as a model. All of us have the experience of sleep. Your individuality, your world experience, the subject-object division are not there in deep sleep. There is no concept of time or space. You do not know where you are or what the time is. In fact you are not manifest in deep sleep. In Sanskrit the unmanifest is known as *avyakta*. So, the individual is *avyakta*, not manifest, in deep sleep. If you wake up from sleep, completely wake up, then you are with this world. You have to deal with the objects of your senses. If, however, you are only half awake, then it is called the dream state. This dream experience can help you understand Īśvara's manifestation.

'Dream' model to understand the identity between the maker and material

In a dream, you are the maker, the author of all that is there in the dream world. The dream world is born of your knowledge. In a dream you cannot create an object that you have never seen before. What you think of is always what you know. You cannot think of what you do not know. If I ask you to think of *gagabugain*, you cannot think of it. Even while awake you cannot think of *gagabugain* much less while dreaming. You may ask me,

"Swamiji, what is *gagabugain*?" If I knew, I would not use it as an example. I have been keeping this group of syllables for a number of years to teach the fact that you cannot think of an object you do not know.

So, in a dream you cannot see something that is totally unknown. You may say that last night, in your dream, you saw a man with two horns. It is true that you have not seen such a person in real life, but you see such people in Star Wars, in cartoons, and science fiction. You have, of course, seen an animal with horns and you have seen human beings. In the dream both the man and the horns became jumbled, and hence, you saw a man with horns. Therefore, in your dream, you create only what you know. You think of space, space appears; you think of time, time is there; you think of the sun, the earth and the people; all of them are there because you think of them, and they are there the instant you think of them.

The material for the dream world is not borrowed from somewhere outside. This is an amazing *śakti*, power. It is not mere imagination. In imagination, you know that you are imagining. In fantasies you are aware that you are fantasising, whereas a dream is not a fantasy. The dream objects have a degree of reality. In the dream, the man who is chasing you is real. Your running, falling, and having cramps are also real.

You are the intelligent cause for the dream world because you have the knowledge. You are also the material to create that dream world. Therefore, being the material cause for the dream world, you, the maker, are not away from the dream world. In other words, the maker can be without the dream world, but the dream world cannot be without the maker. In our model of the dream, the dream space, air, fire, water, earth and everything else that is there, is you. Therefore, you are all pervasive in the dream. The dream world is not separate from you. The consciousness that is you is the consciousness in which space, time, the world, every person, body, every cell, the subject, the object, exist. It is one complete live organic whole. This is your experience. Waking up, you are able to relate this. If, in the dream, someone were to realise this fact, it would be marvellous. You could learn Vedanta in dream. Unfortunately, in dream you do not have your freewill because you are not a complete person. You are only half awake, but that is good enough to create a world for yourself.

Then, when you are awake you confront this world, which is exactly like the world you created in your dream, created from the standpoint of the knowledge implied in making that world. It is a manifestation because, in dream, you manifest as space, as time and as whatever else that is there. Similarly, Īśvara, being the intelligent and material cause for the creation, manifests as space, time, sun, moon, stars and everything that is here. This is the reason why we approach any form with reverence.

Every form is Īśvara

Every form is a manifestation of Īśvara. When every form is Īśvara you can invoke him in any given form. You can invoke Īśvara as a male, as a female and both as male and female, father and mother. Therefore, you have no problems in offering your prayers to any form. One has to understand his or her culture. It is a profound culture, although, as yet, we have not understood its profundity.

There are people who say that we worship idols. They also say that we even worship milestones. If somebody is able to invoke the Lord in a milestone and offer flowers and worship it, should you not walk miles to see that person? This vision is not ordinary. Nobody worships an idol. You only worship the Lord whom you understand. Therefore, you can worship the Lord in every form. The 'non-idol' worshippers have removed forms because their religion forbids them from worshipping an image. They do not realise that they have lost a great deal. For us, every form is the Lord, whereas for some others, the Lord created the world expressly for human beings. Consequently, they do not respect other forms. All the environmental problems are due to this lack of reverence for form.

Since we see the Lord in every form, we can worship even an animal. Unfortunately, we are immediately labelled as animists. What is wrong in worshipping animals? In fact, they are worthy of worship because they have no ego. You can even worship another person, except that the person has his or her own ego with all its resultant problems. Therefore, you cannot worship another person. However, we can and do worship a saint because he is presumed to have resolved that ego.

Some people criticise us saying that we worship Gods with forms, with families, with preferences, and that we transform them to suit our individual tastes. There is absolutely nothing wrong in our choice of forms. In fact, it helps us to relate better with the Lord. Carl Jung appreciated this aspect of our culture. He appreciated the fact that we are able to imbue our gods with likes and dislikes and still worship them. It means that we are able to accept realities. Those who oppose forms do not have even a ritualistic prayer. They cannot perform a *pūjā*. The ritualistic prayer is very effective because in doing it, you are complete. You physicalise your emotions there. When you physicalise your emotions, when you express them, the emotions become real.

We can invoke Īśvara in any one form. For us, everything is a form. Language is a form. The script is a form. Your dress is a form and your greeting each other is nothing but a form. In the court when you address the judge as 'Your Lordship,' it is nothing but form. In fact, every thought is a form. There is no formless thought. When you think of a pot, it is a form. It is form, all the way. The whole of life is lived in forms.

People who criticise the worship of forms do not understand this vision. They do not realise that their altars and prayers are also forms. Moreover, when they say that we should worship only one God, they have a problem. They say they should not worship other Gods.

Everything that is here is Īśvara's manifestation. Then how do you look at and understand this manifestation of

Īśvara, who is all knowledge? Space and time are not separate from Īśvara, the Lord. Anything that is in space and time—the sun, moon, stars, your body, mind, your senses, the earth, the elements, the elementals and everything that is here—is not separate from Īśvara. We look upon even death as Īśvara, as Lord Yama. We are not afraid of death. We worship death.

Īśvara is one total order

We see an order in this manifestation. Suppose a flower does not remain always a flower. If it suddenly changes into a scorpion, you cannot wear the flower on your hair. The head itself might turn into something else! There will be confusion. In the creation, however, we find that there is an order, both at the macro level and at the micro level. If a flower is definable as a flower, there is an order; that is why knowledge is possible. We can look at the whole manifestation in the form of various orders.

Īśvara is manifest in the form of physical order, the physical universe which includes all the forces, geology, thermodynamics, your physical body and its behaviour and so on. When you study physics, you are in touch with Īśvara. Besides the inert objects, there are the life forms that imply certain possibilities. They form the biological order; trees and plants also come under this order. When you study biology you are studying Īśvara. Then, there is *prāṇa,* the life force, in every living organism. The functions of this life force that govern health or ill health come under the physiological order, which is another manifestation of Īśvara. A study of physiology would be a study of Īśvara.

The psychological order, including the memory, is yet another manifestation of Īśvara. The human behaviour is within this order, since all our responses are memory based. Then there is the cognitive order by which you understand all these orders. It is because of the cognitive order that you can distinguish knowledge, error, the right conclusion and so on. Epistemology is based on this order. The cognitive order also includes an aspect of memory. That is why you are able to recognise the person you had met earlier, in the recent or remote past.

There is no distance between one order and another. Where there is a physical order, there is a biological order too. There is no spatial distance between physiology or biology or psychology. Thus Īśvara, who is all knowledge, is in the form of one *mahā* order, total order. In this order, I am given the freewill to desire, to choose, to act. The result, however, is taken care of by the laws, that is Īśvara. That is why you cannot blame the order, the laws. If you stick your finger in the fire it will burn. The laws produce the results of actions and Īśvara is in the form of the laws.

The laws include the laws of *dharma* and *adharma*. What you do not want others to do to you is *adharma*, what you want others to do to you is *dharma*. Human beings did not create this order, but we sense it and that is why it is universal. You do not see gravitation, but you sense it and so do the animals and birds. Without the knowledge of gravitation, no monkey can jump from tree to tree. Well, you sense gravitation because it exists. It exists in your mind. *Dharma* also does not lie outside you. It is in your mind, manifesting in your life, manifesting in your desires and actions.

The fact that you have desires, that you want to fulfil them, that you can plan and execute an action, is a privilege. These are all privileges. It is also a fact that there are four possible results to an action. That is the reason why you are prayerful. Before you start anything you always pray, because you do not know what the outcome is going to be. In India, you pray before starting the car. The prayer is meant to avoid undesirable things. You see the green light and you proceed. The assumption is that the other person has seen the red light. Unfortunately for you, he sees too many lights. How do you control that? Therefore, you say a prayer; this is our culture. Now you can understand why we have ritualistic and other forms of prayers.

Every result is prasāda coming from Īśvara

If all that is here is Īśvara, then with this understanding, you can have a proper attitude. All the laws are manifestations of Īśvara, are not separate from Īśvara. Therefore, when you say the laws produce the results, it means Īśvara produces the results. Every result comes from Īśvara. Since you have the opportunity, the privilege of growing in this culture, you have an inbuilt attitude that has grown upon you; that is the attitude of glad acceptance, *prasāda* attitude.

Anything that comes from Īśvara is *prasāda. Prasāda* can be anything. It can be a *laddoo,* or a sugar crystal; it can be the leaf of a *tulasi,* basil, or *vilva,* bael, given in the temple. It can be a home that is given to you. It can be your child that you are blessed with. Your body itself is a *prasāda.* Your set of senses is *prasāda.* What is given is *prasāda* because it comes from Īśvara. Please tell me what is not given? Everything is given. That you can put things together, that capacity is given. Therefore, anything that comes to you is *prasāda. Prasāda* also means assimilation of facts. A person who can assimilate facts and go ahead with his or her life is successful. Assimilating facts is done with the attitude that everything is *prasāda.* If you say that you cannot accept a lesser result as *prasāda,* and that you need the other result, then go ahead and work for it. However, you must ensure that you do not succumb to the emotional pressures created by your likes and dislikes, and follow *dharma.*

Generally, it so happens that whatever you like to do is what is not to be done, a wrong action, and whatever you do not like to do is what is to be done, a right action, like going to work early in the morning. What you want to do is not to go. What you have to do is go to work. Therefore, what is success in life?

Successful living is when you go by what is to be done, with a prayerful attitude, with understanding. In the beginning, there is a conflict between what you do not like to do and what is to be done. Yet, you are able to pull yourself together and do what is to be done at the cost of your dislike, *dveṣa.* It is the same with reference to what should not be done, when it is exactly what you want to do. Here again, with an understanding, you conform to what is right, and avoid doing what is not to be done at the cost of your desire, *rāga*. This is called *kauśala,* discretion.

When you practice what is right, even though you do not like doing it, and avoid what is wrong, even though you want to do it, you slowly change. Later, you find yourself in a position where what is to be done is what you like to do and what is not to be done is what you do not like to do. That is, indeed, a successful life.

When you do the right thing, you conform to *dharma* that is Īśvara. Lord Kṛṣṇa says, "In a human being I am in the form of desire that does not transgress *dharma.*" When you transgress *dharma,* you are rubbing against Īśvara. When you rub against *dharma,* you are not intelligent. You are just a loser. When you conform to *dharma,* then you are in tune, in harmony, with Īśvara.

So, by doing your duty, *svakarma,* what is proper, what is appropriate at a given time, place and situation, you are worshipping Īśvara. You are the most successful person, *siddhiṁ vindati mānavaḥ*. It means that such a person is spontaneously good and is successful. This is successful living. There is so much to own up, there is so much to enjoy, if one achieves this success.

Oṁ tat sat

Books by Swami Dayananda

Public Talk 1 Living Intelligently
Public Talk 2 Successful Living
Muṇḍakopaniṣad Vol - 1
Muṇḍakopaniṣad Vol - 2
Freedom from Helplessness
Living versus Getting On
The Value of Values
Insights
Action and Reaction
Exploring Vedanta
Bhagavad Gītā (Text with roman transliteration and English translation)
The Fundamental Problem
The Problem is You, The Solution is You
The Purpose of Prayer
Vedanta 24x7
Freedom
Crisis Management
Surrender and Freedom
The Need for Personal Reorganisation
Freedom in Relationship
Bhagavad Gītā Home Study Course Hardbound (Vol 1-4)
Bhagavad Gītā Home Study Course Softbound (Vol 1-4)

Also available at :

ARSHA VIDYA CENTRE
(RESEARCH • PUBLICATION)
32/4 Sir Desika Road
Mylapore Chennai 600 004
Telefax : 044 - 2499 7131
Email : avrandpc@gmail.com

ARSHA VIDYA GURUKULAM
Anaikatti P.O.
Coimbatore 641 108
Ph : 0422 - 2657001
Fax : 0422 - 2657002
Email : arsha1@vsnl.com

ARSHA VIDYA GURUKULAM
P.O.Box 1059.
Pennsylvania
PA 18353, USA.
Ph : 001-570-992-2339
Email : avp@epix.net

ARSHA VIDYA PITHAM
SWAMI DAYANANDA ASHRAM
Purani Jhadi, P.B. No. 30
Rishikesh, Uttaranchal 249 201
Telefax : 0135-2430769
Email : dayas@hotmail.com

AND IN ALL THE LEADING BOOKSTORES, INDIA